Adult Coloring Book

# Flowers Mandalas, Garden Designs and Paisley Patterns

*URcoloring*

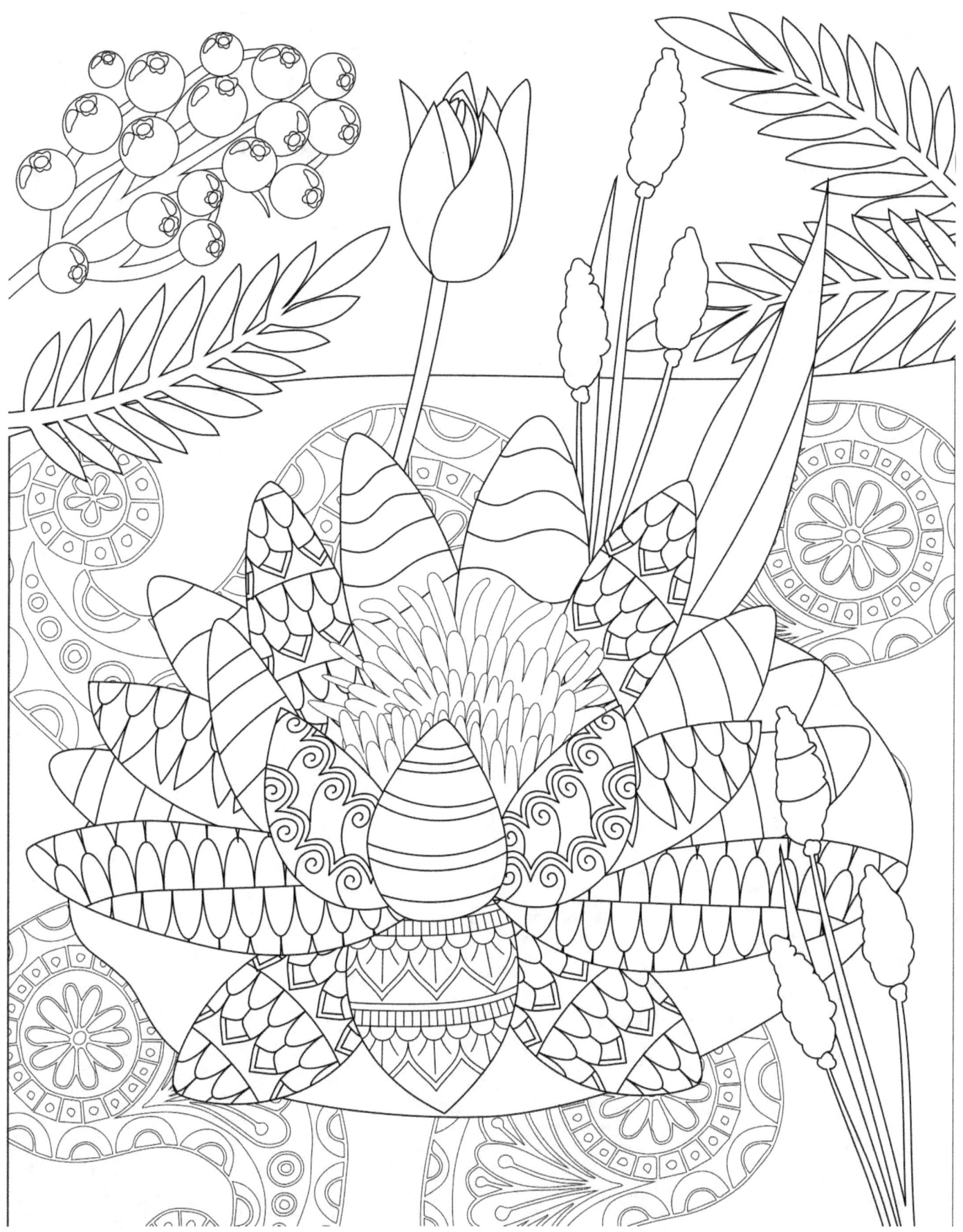

Thank you for purchasing our Coloring Book!
Please leave us a review on Amazon.

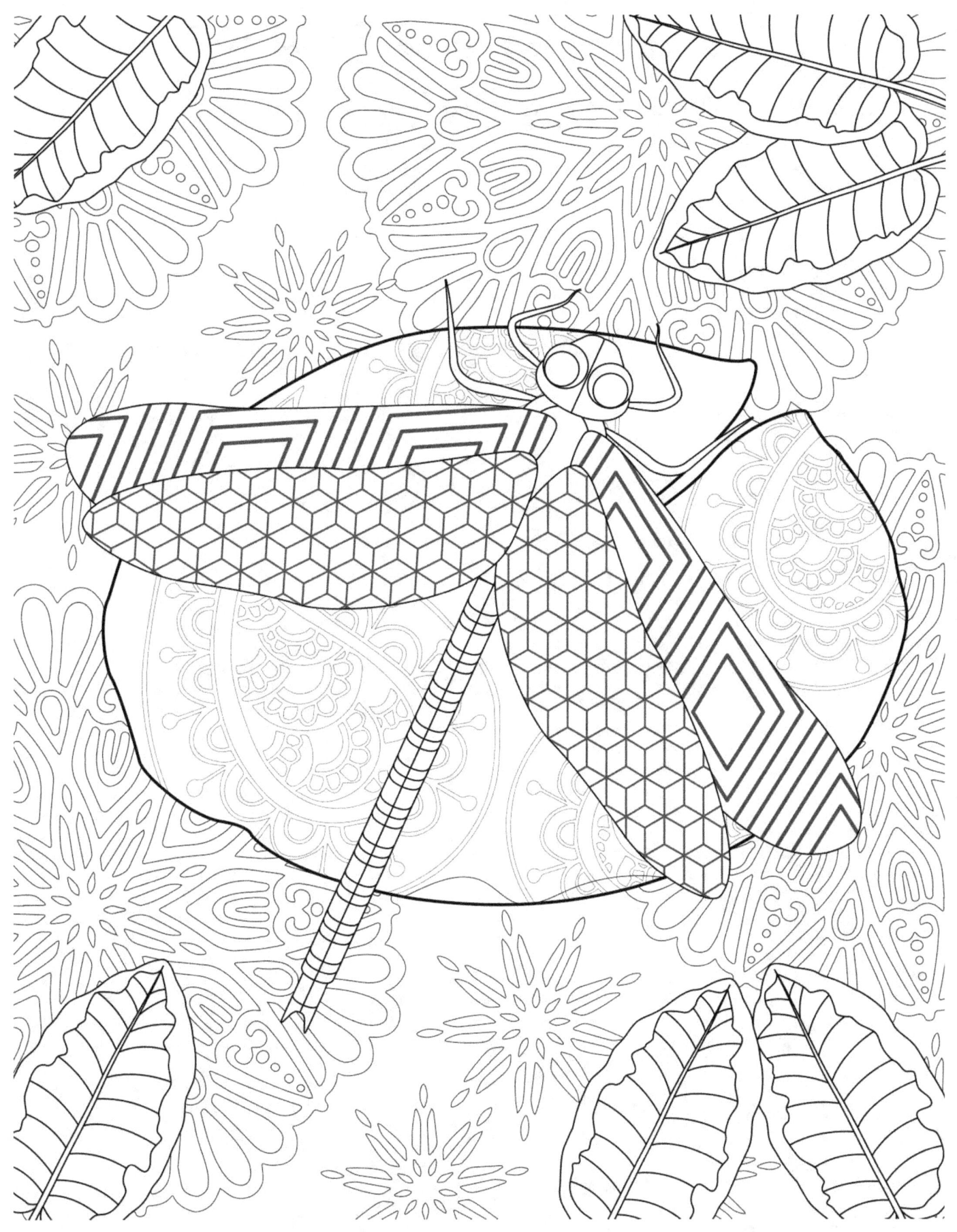

Thank you for purchasing our Coloring Book!
Please leave us a review on Amazon.

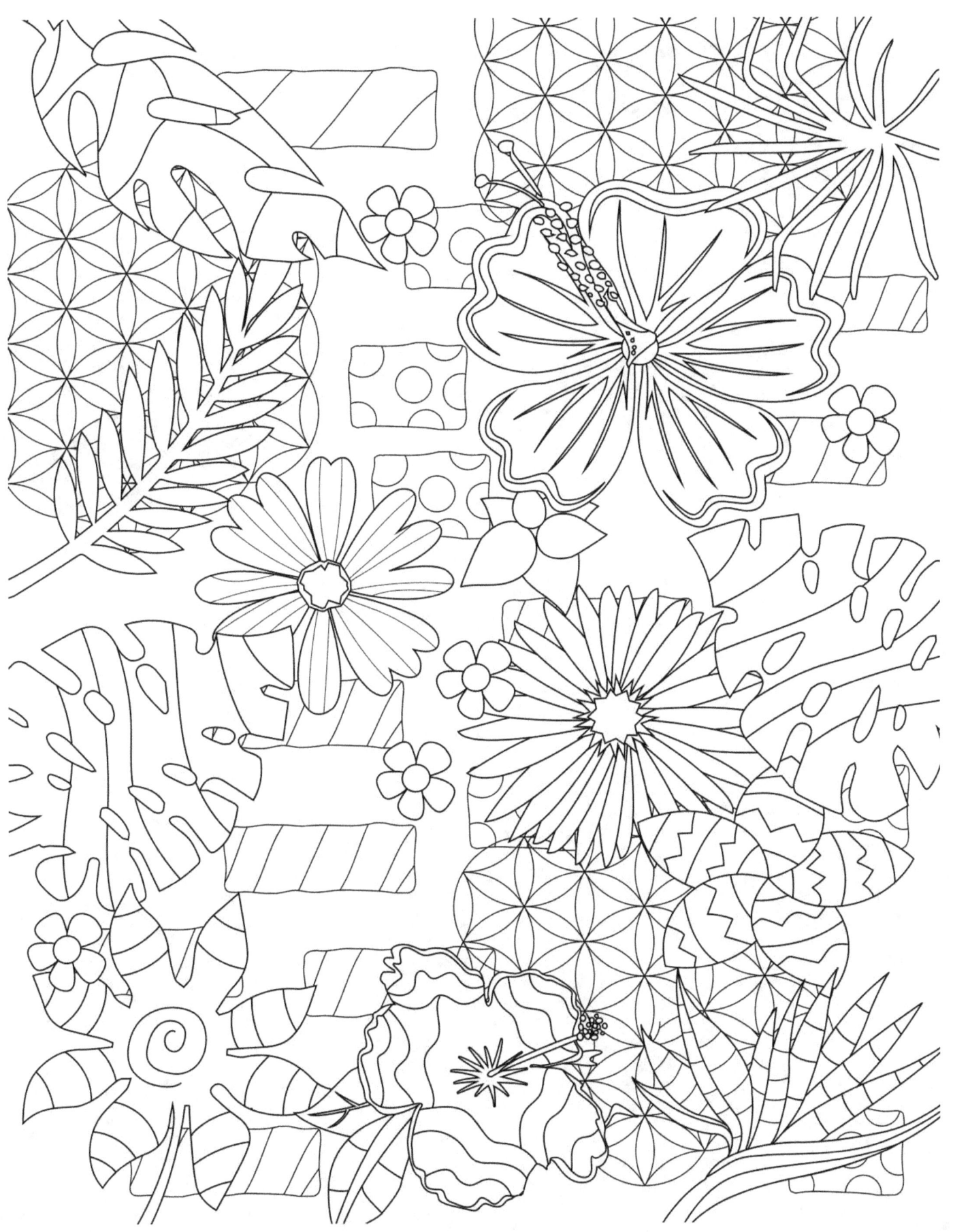

Thank you for purchasing our Coloring Book!
Please leave us a review on Amazon.

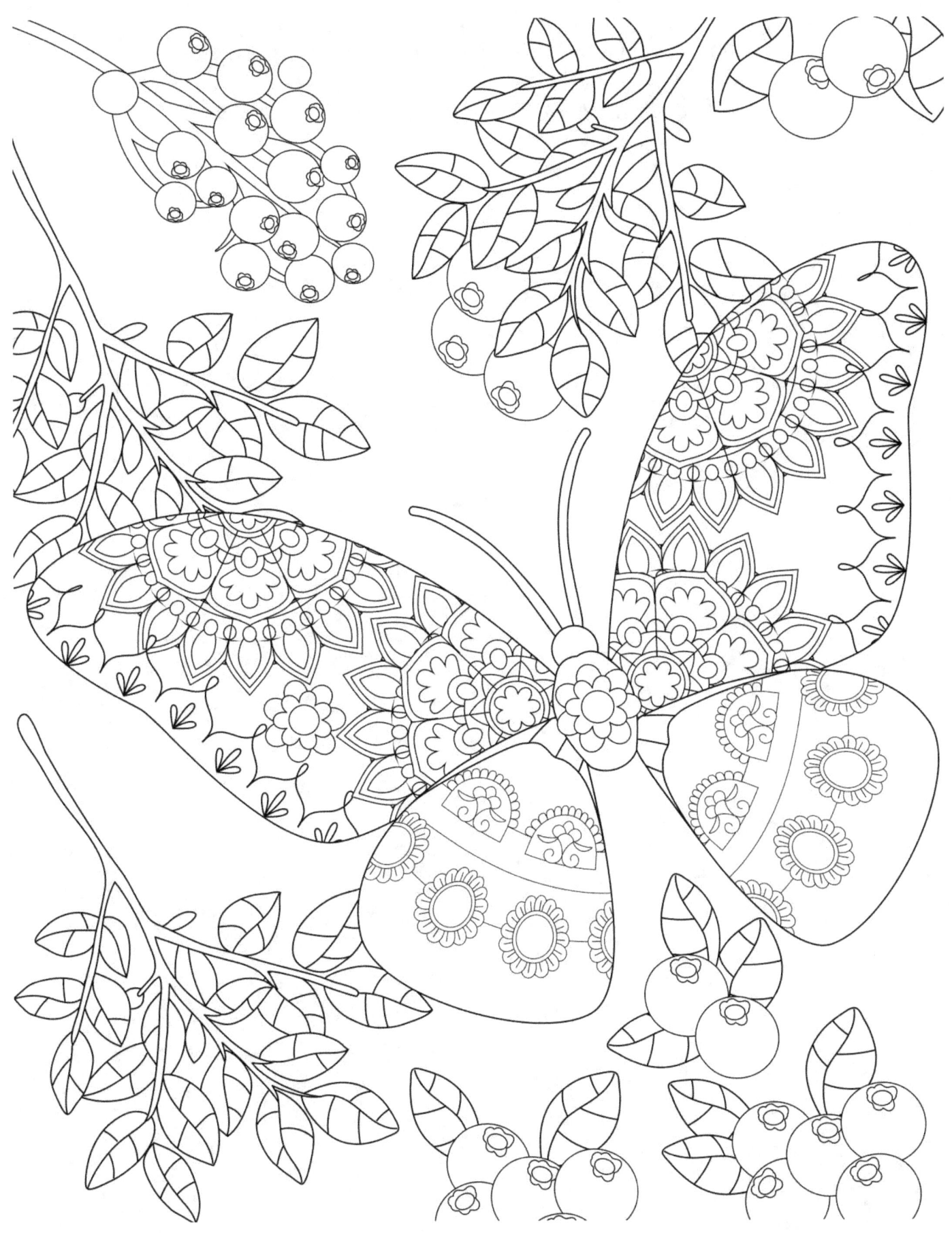

Thank you for purchasing our Coloring Book!
Please leave us a review on Amazon.

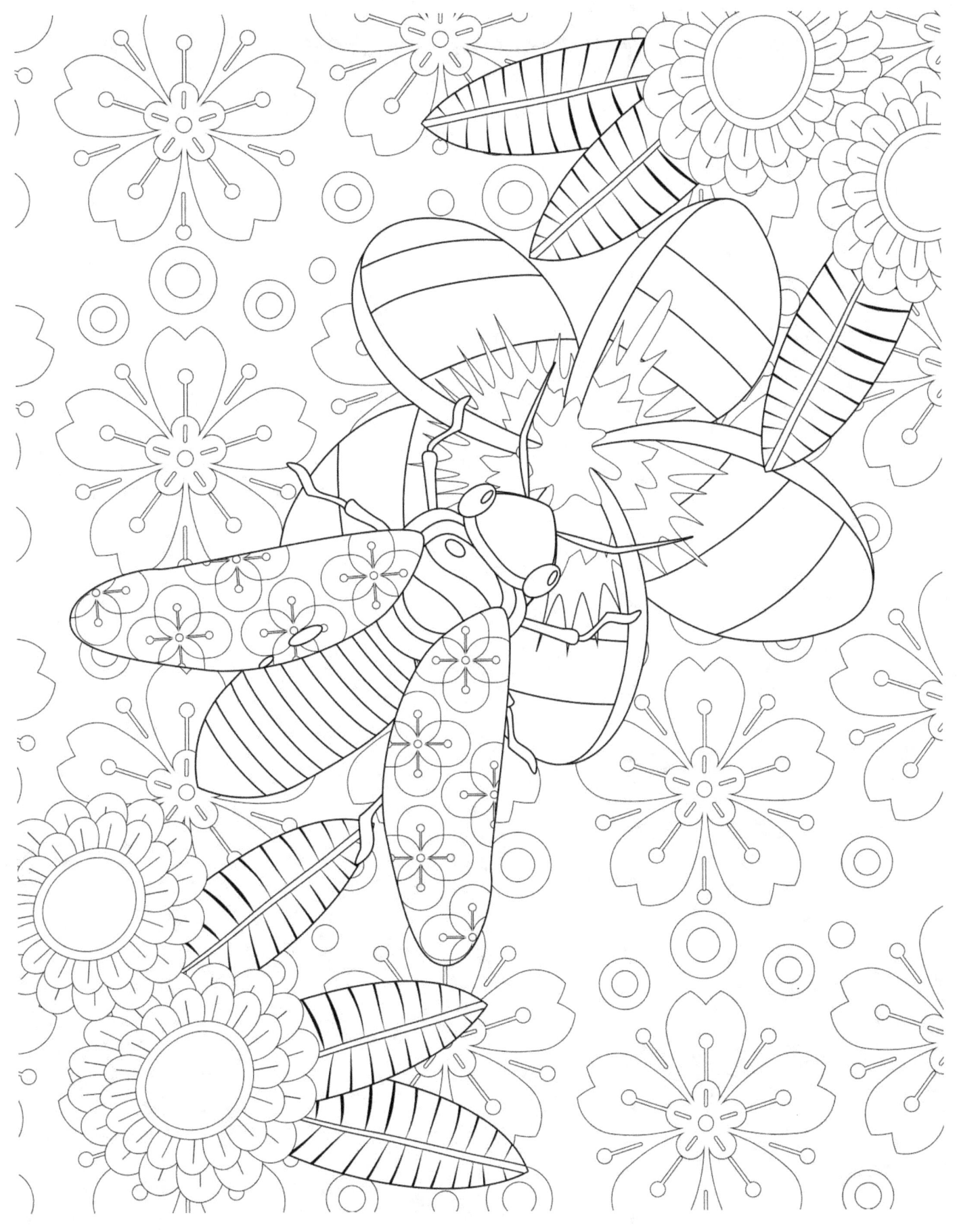

Thank you for purchasing our Coloring Book!
Please leave us a review on Amazon.

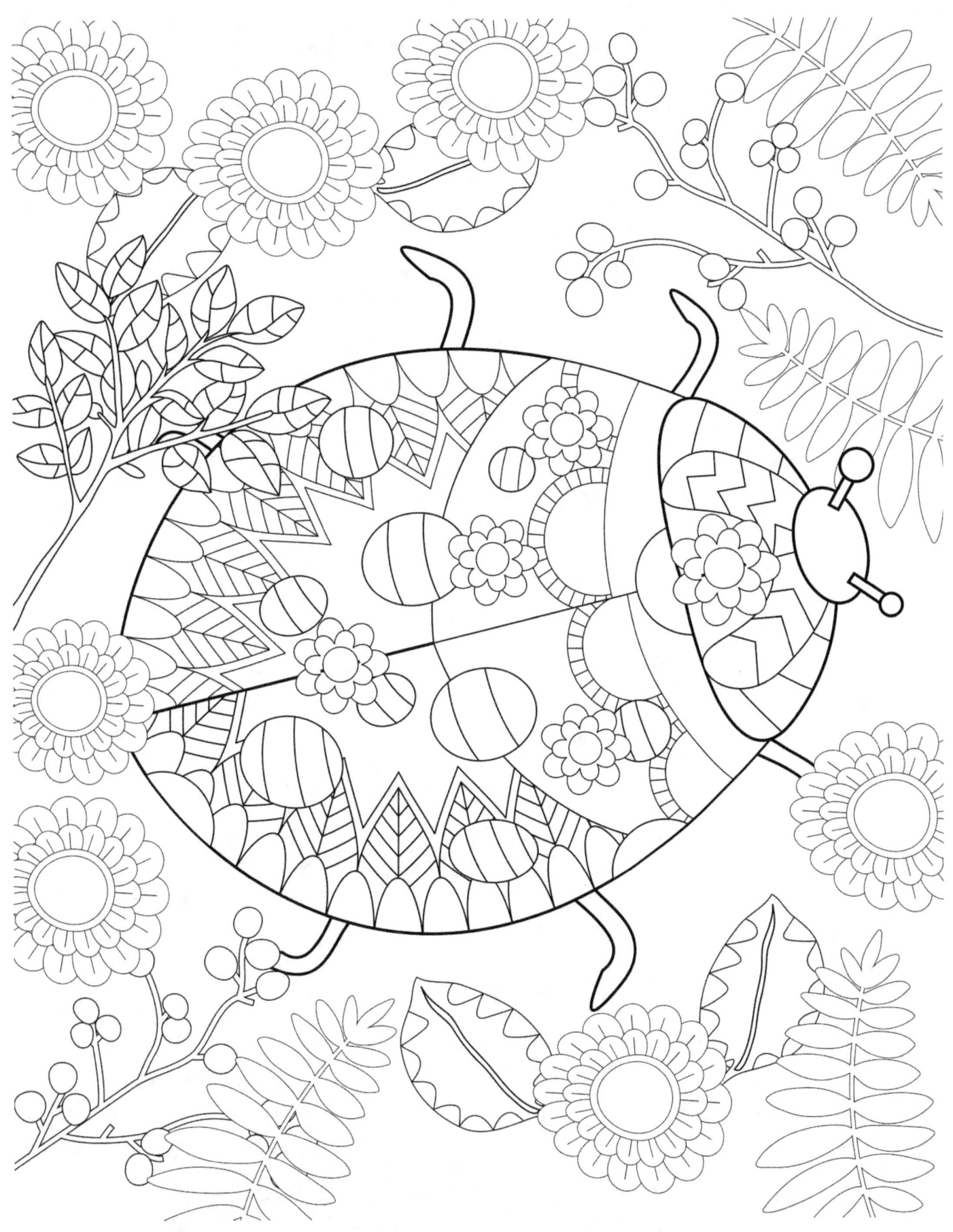

Thank you for purchasing our Coloring Book!
Please leave us a review on Amazon.

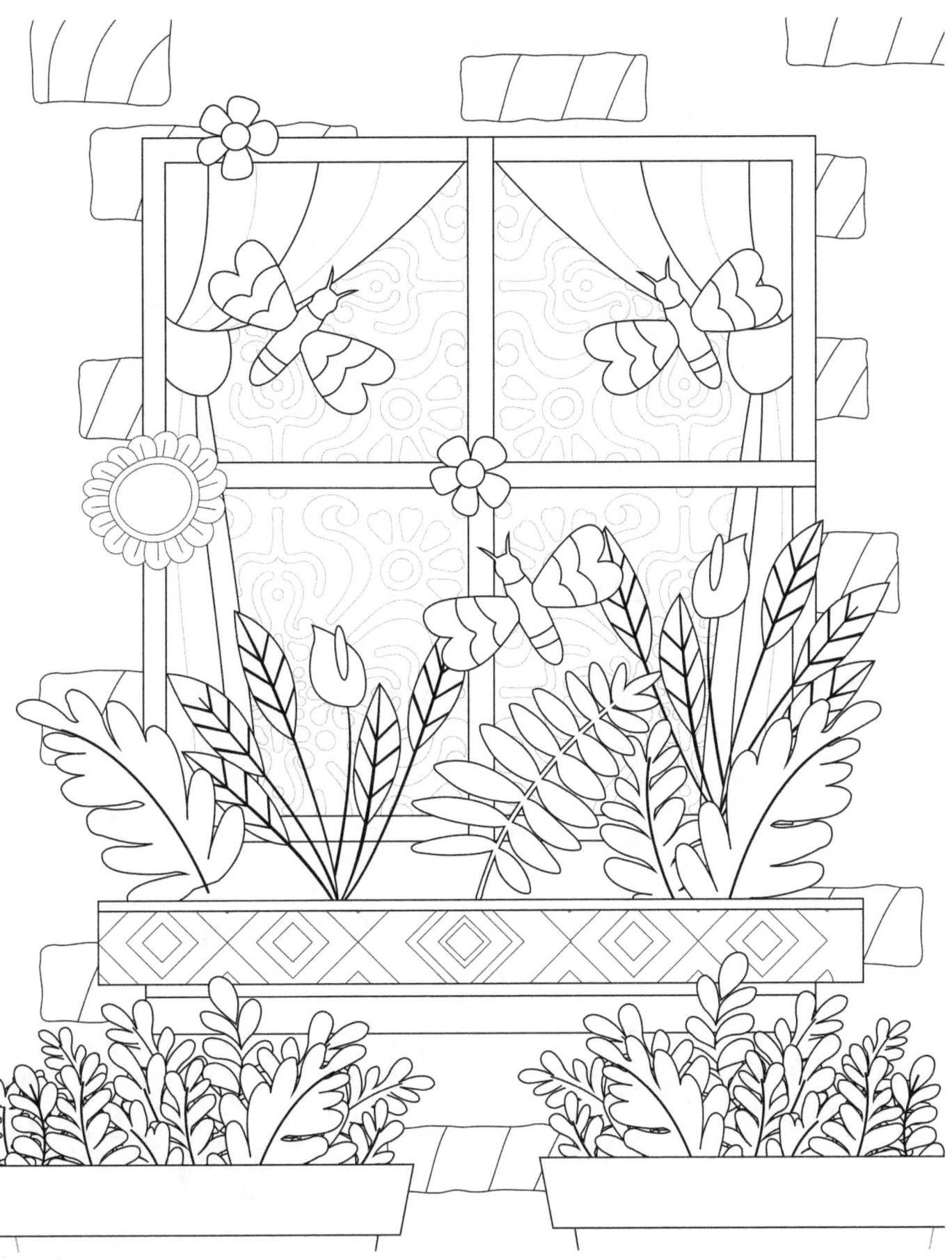

Thank you for purchasing our Coloring Book!
Please leave us a review on Amazon.

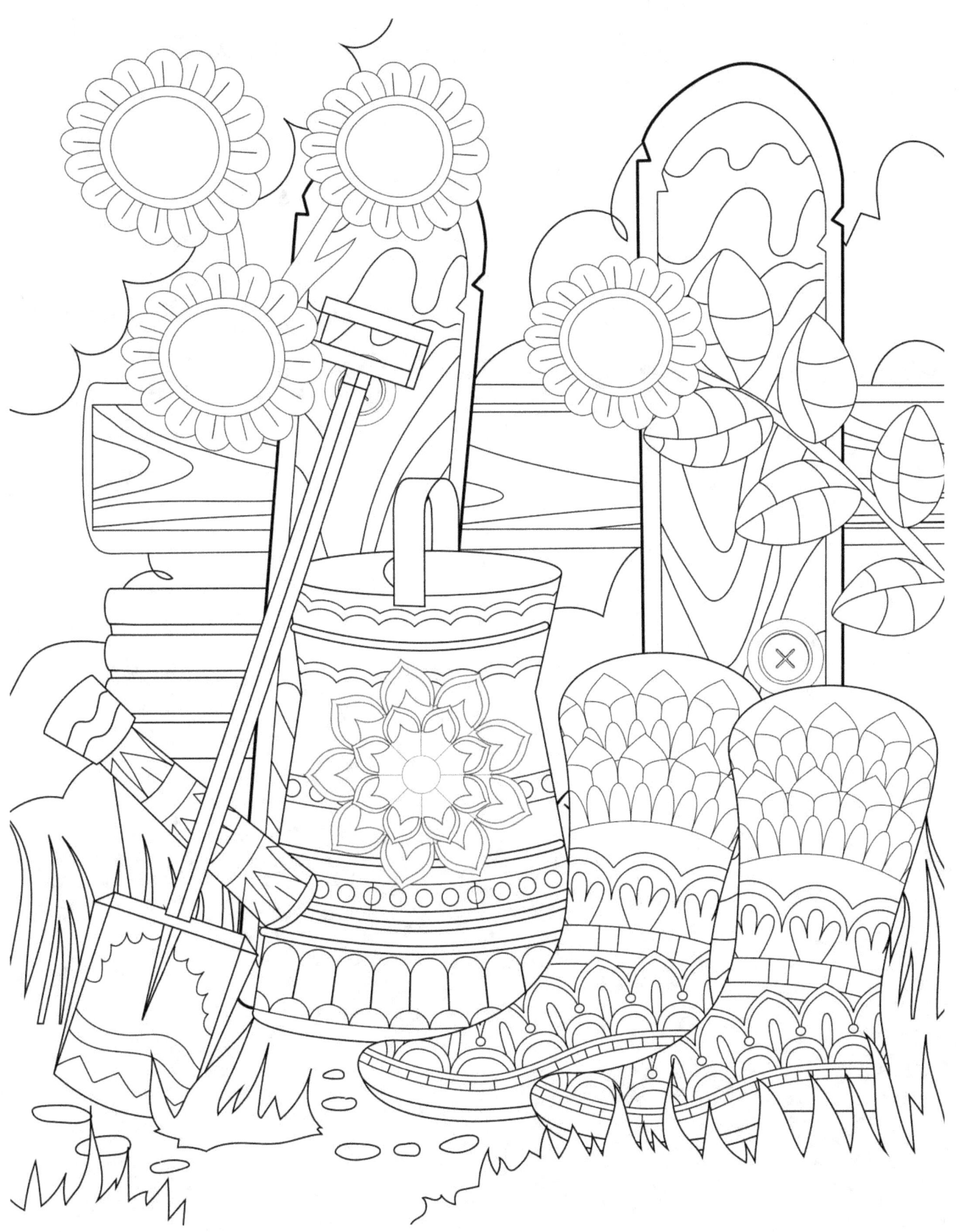

Thank you for purchasing our Coloring Book!
Please leave us a review on Amazon.

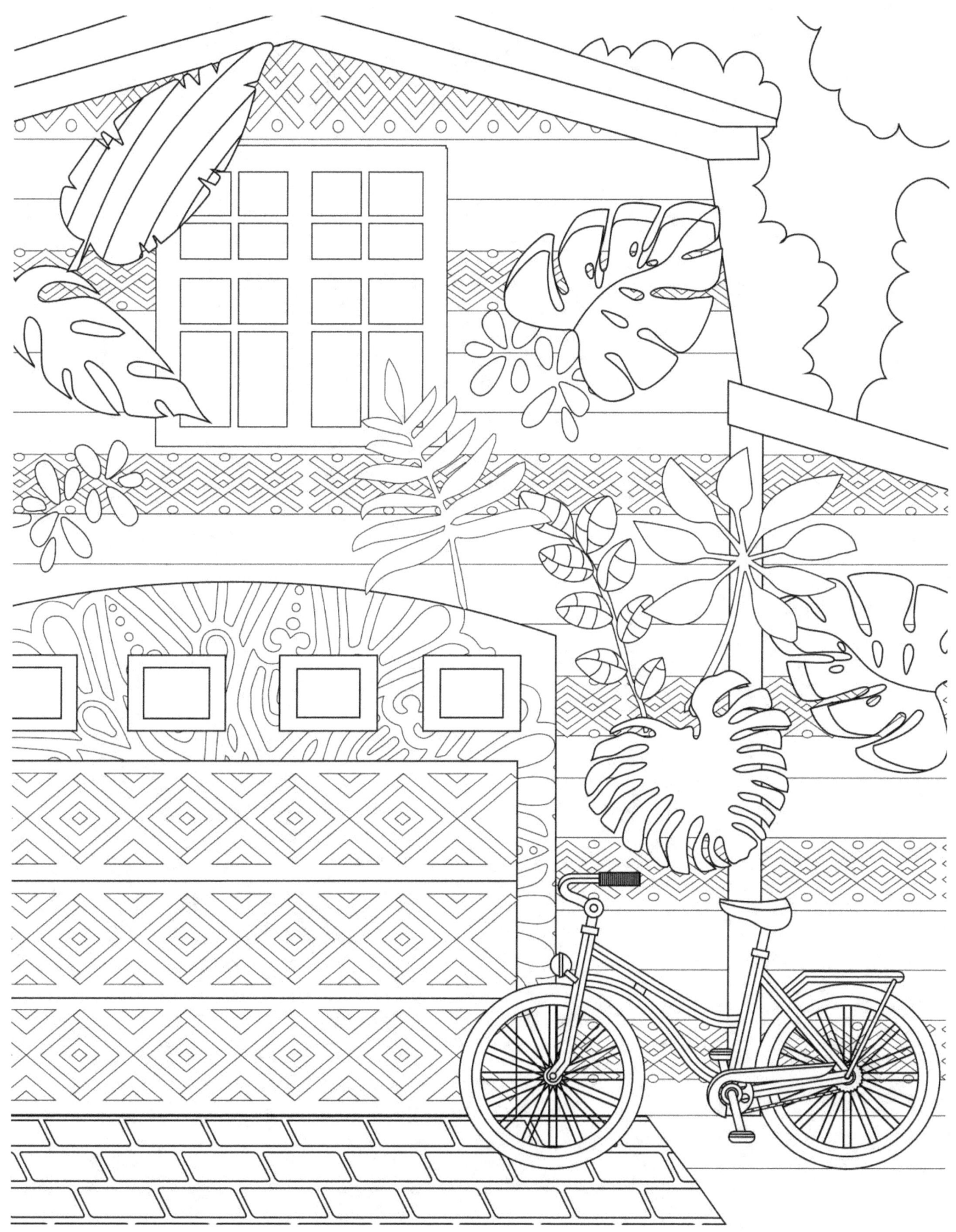

Thank you for purchasing our Coloring Book!
Please leave us a review on Amazon.

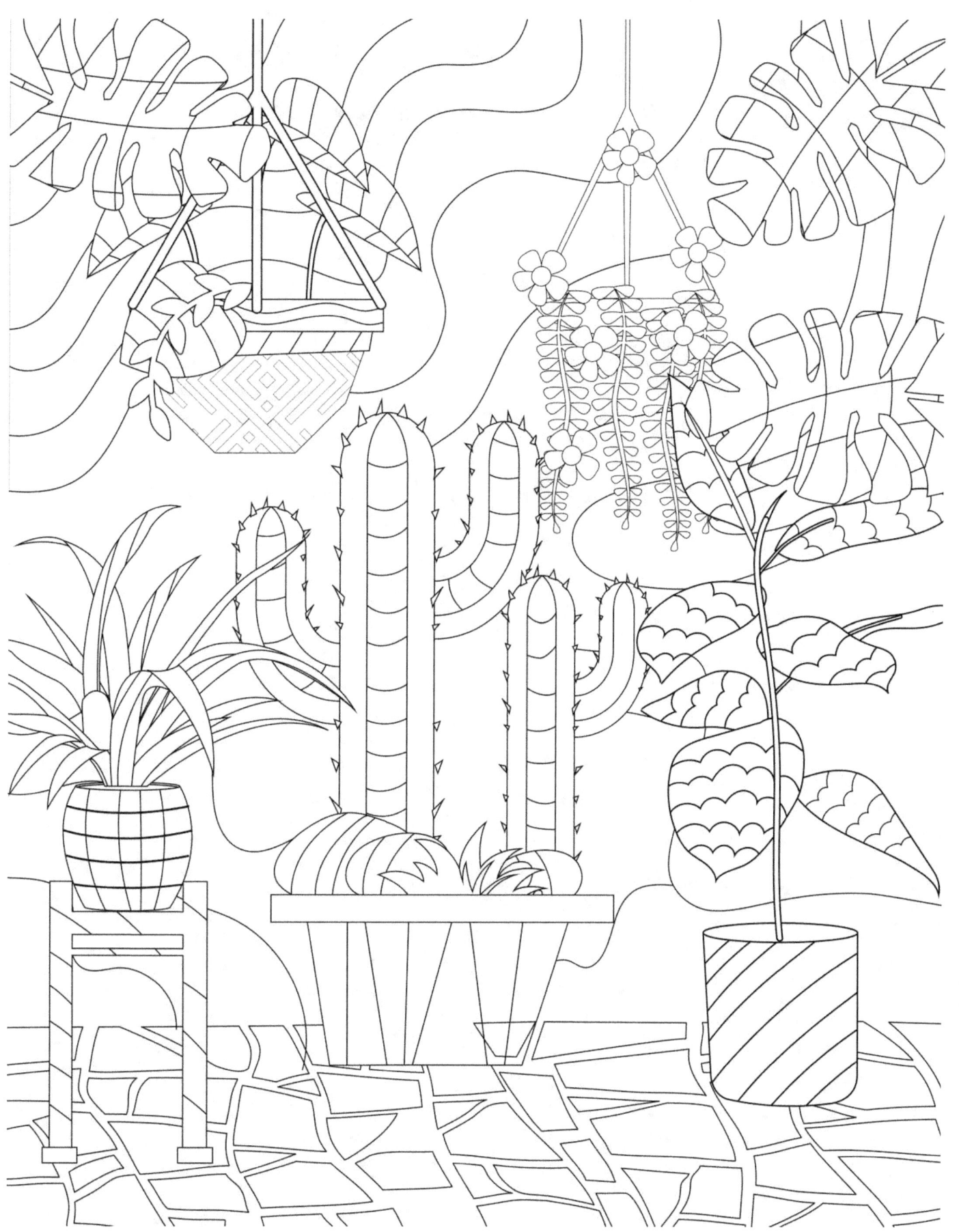

Thank you for purchasing our Coloring Book!
Please leave us a review on Amazon.

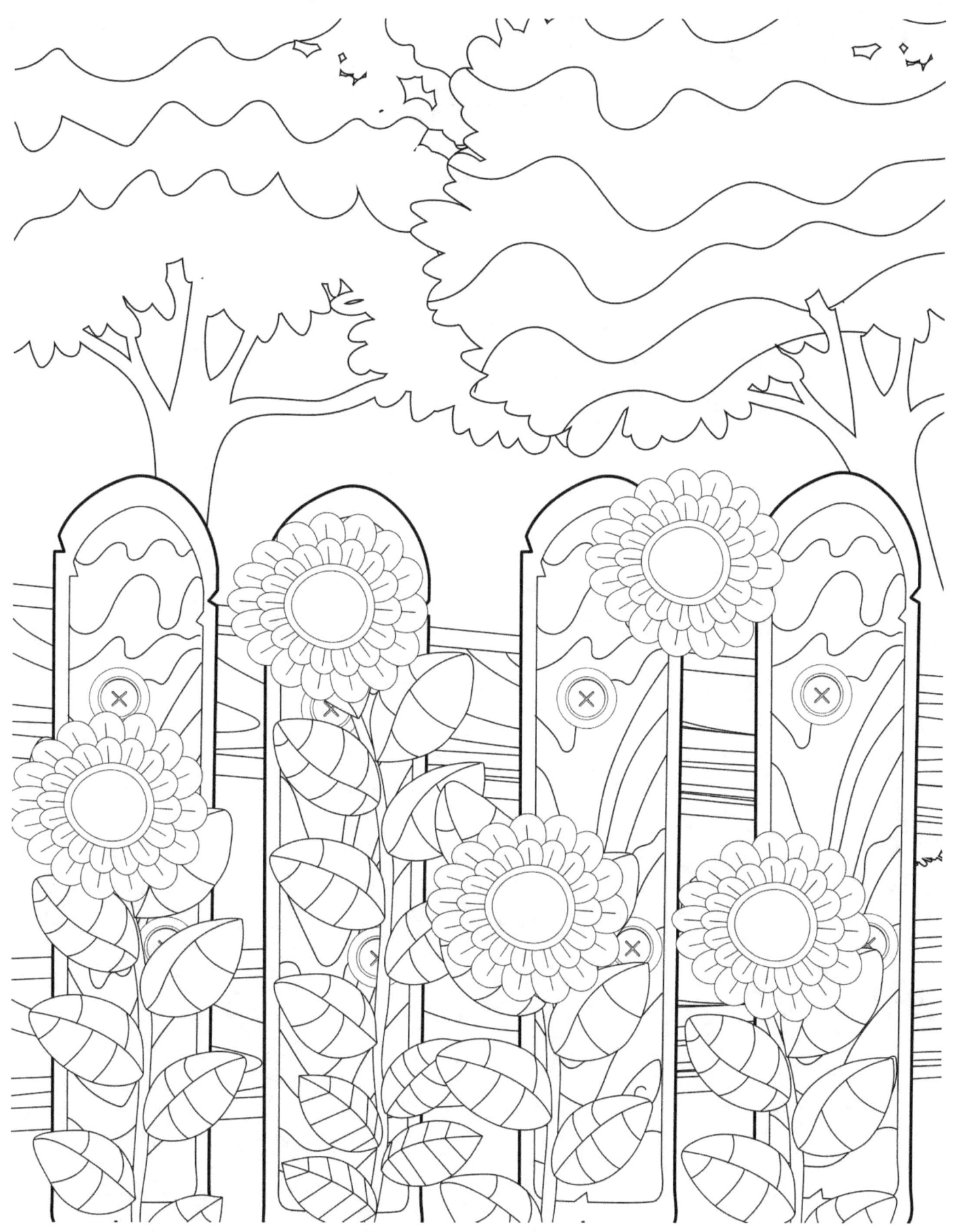

*Thank you for purchasing our Coloring Book!*
*Please leave us a review on Amazon.*

*Thank you for purchasing our Coloring Book!*
*Please leave us a review on Amazon.*

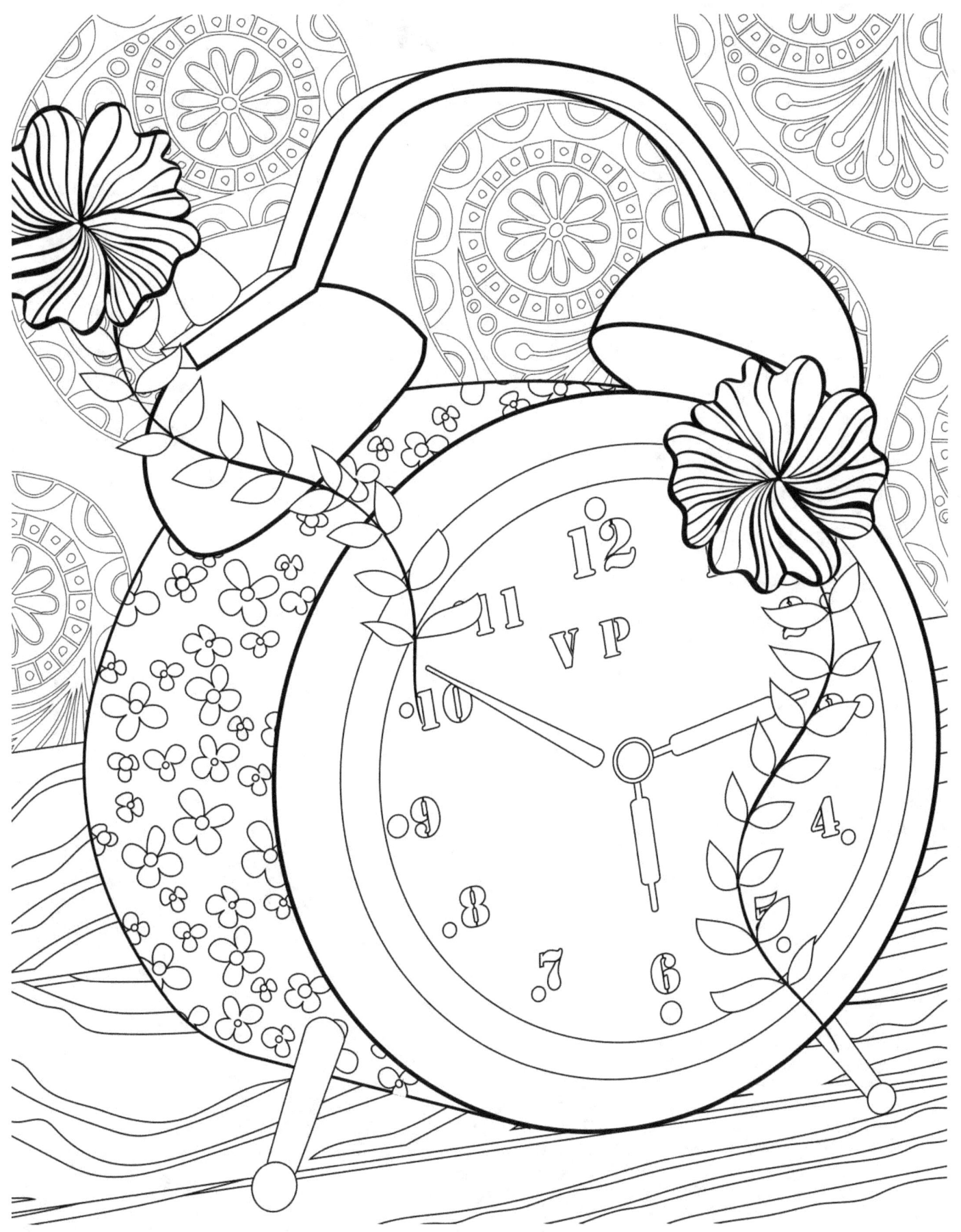

Thank you for purchasing our Coloring Book!
Please leave us a review on Amazon.

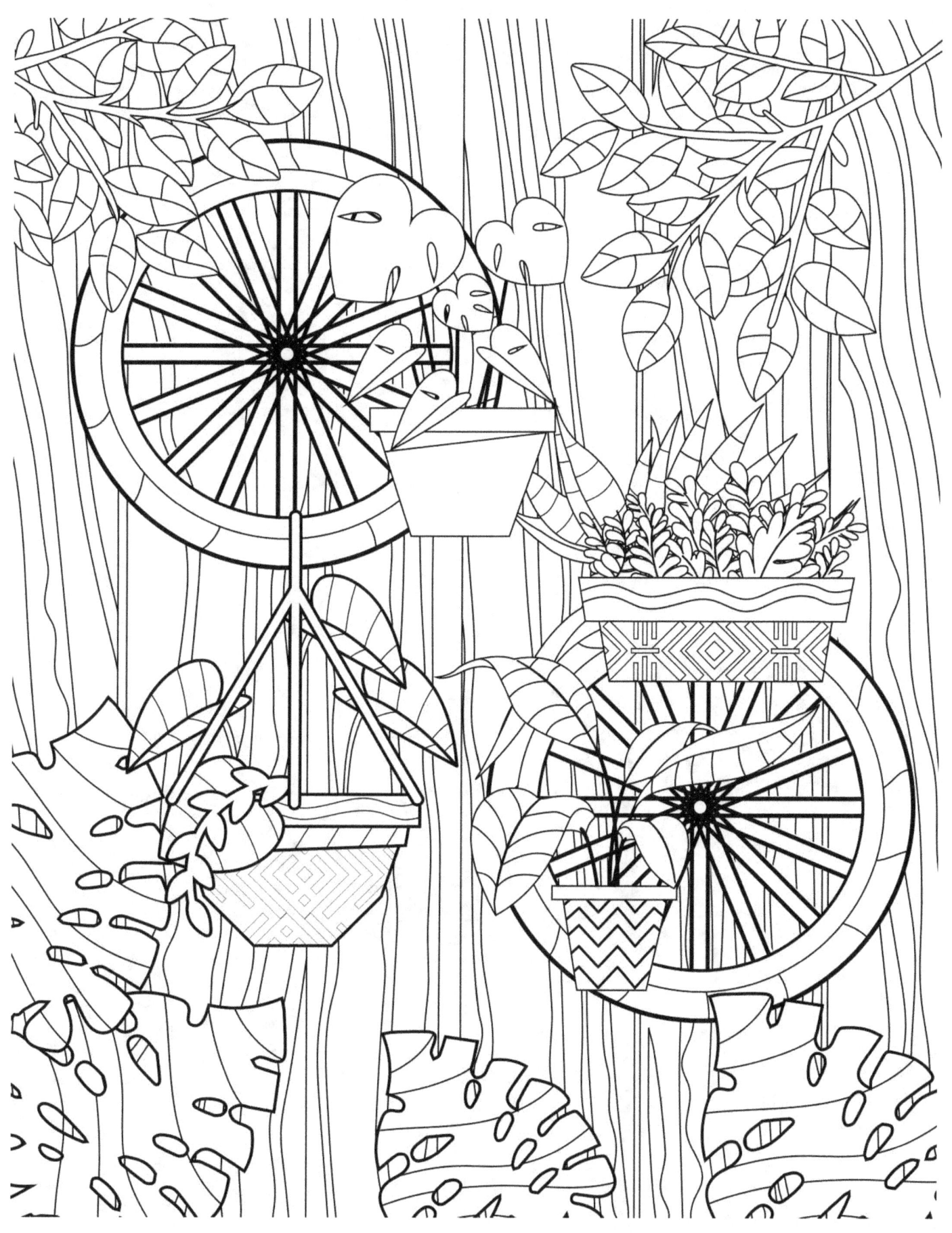

Thank you for purchasing our Coloring Book!
Please leave us a review on Amazon.

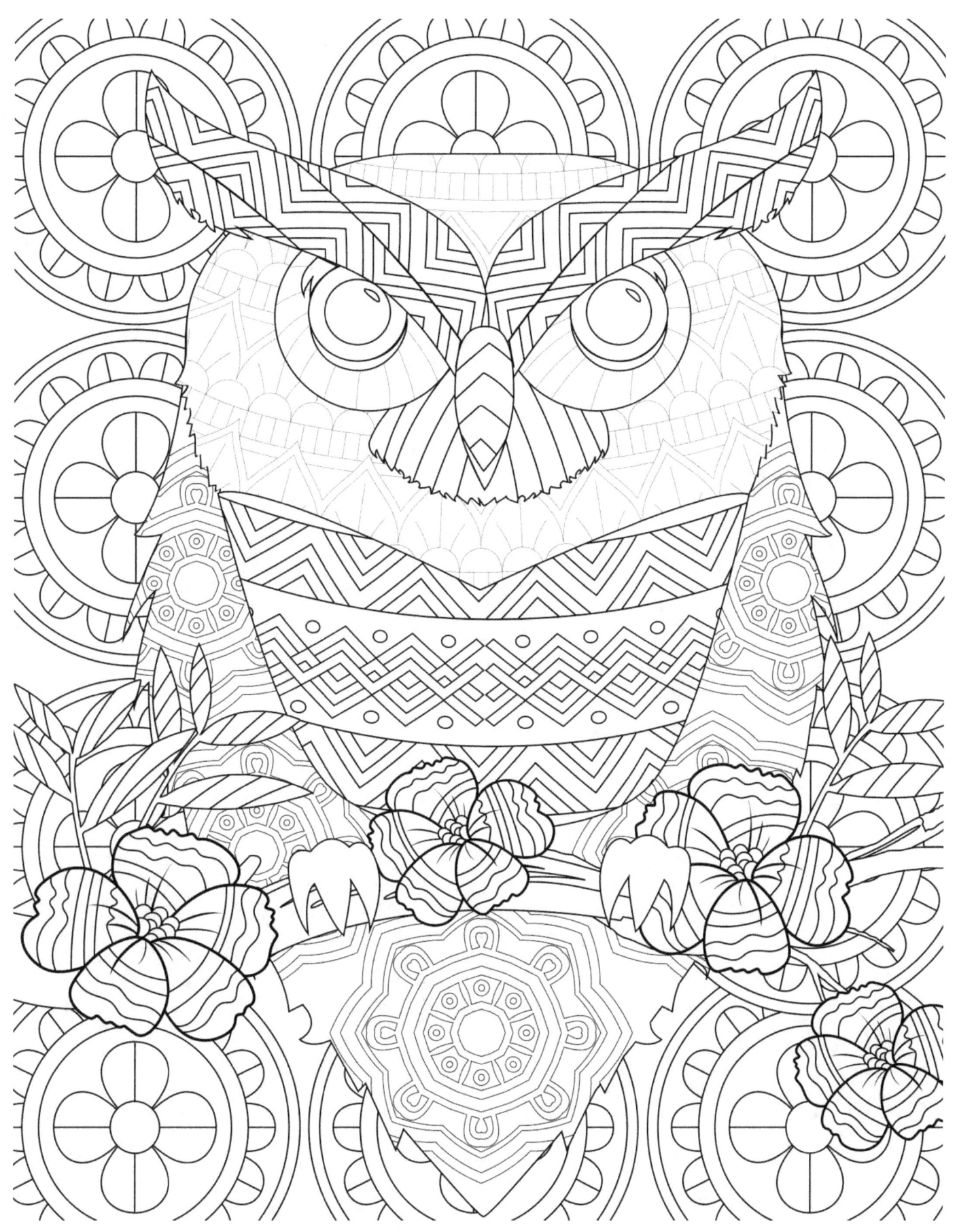

*Thank you for purchasing our Coloring Book!*
*Please leave us a review on Amazon.*

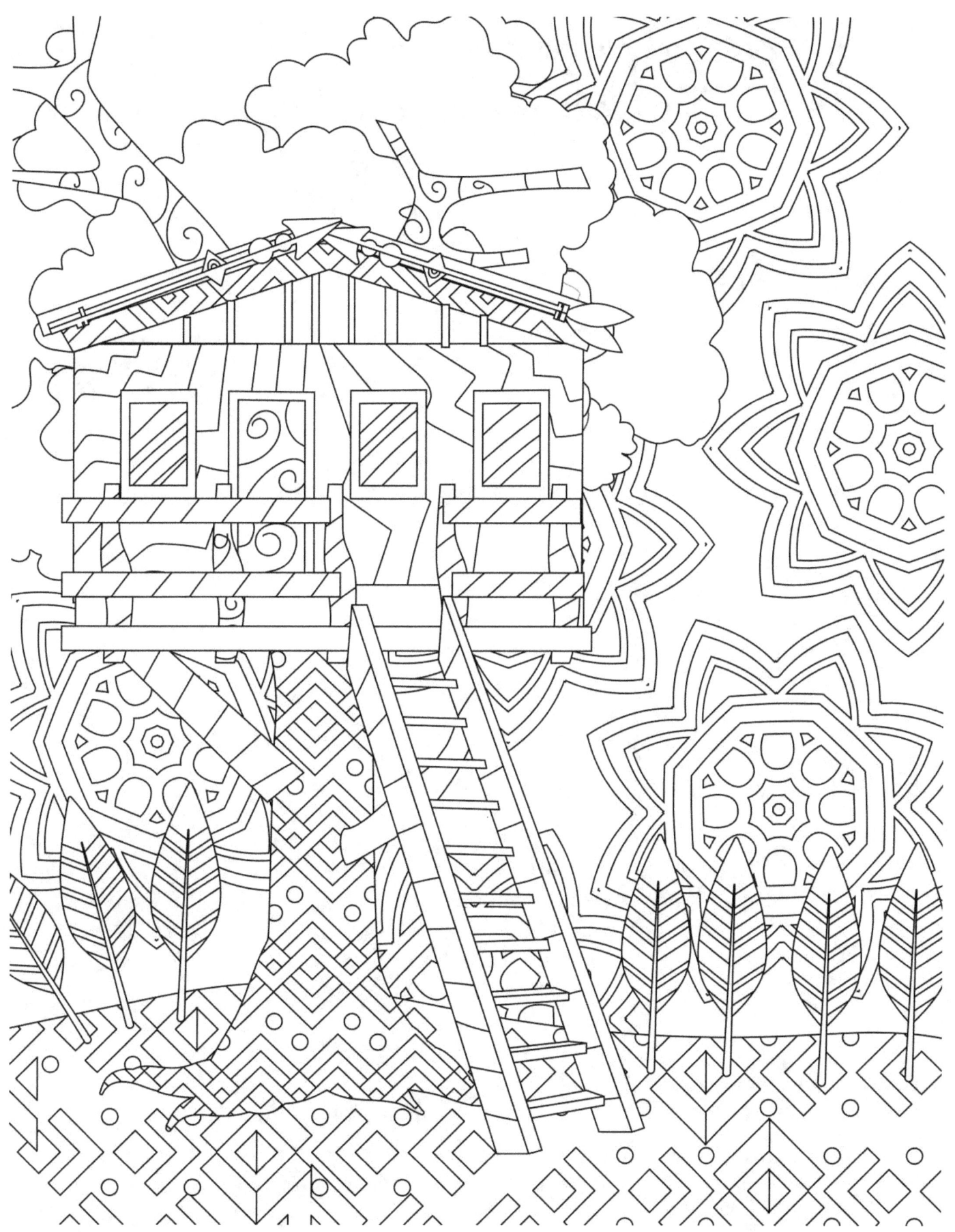

Thank you for purchasing our Coloring Book!
Please leave us a review on Amazon.

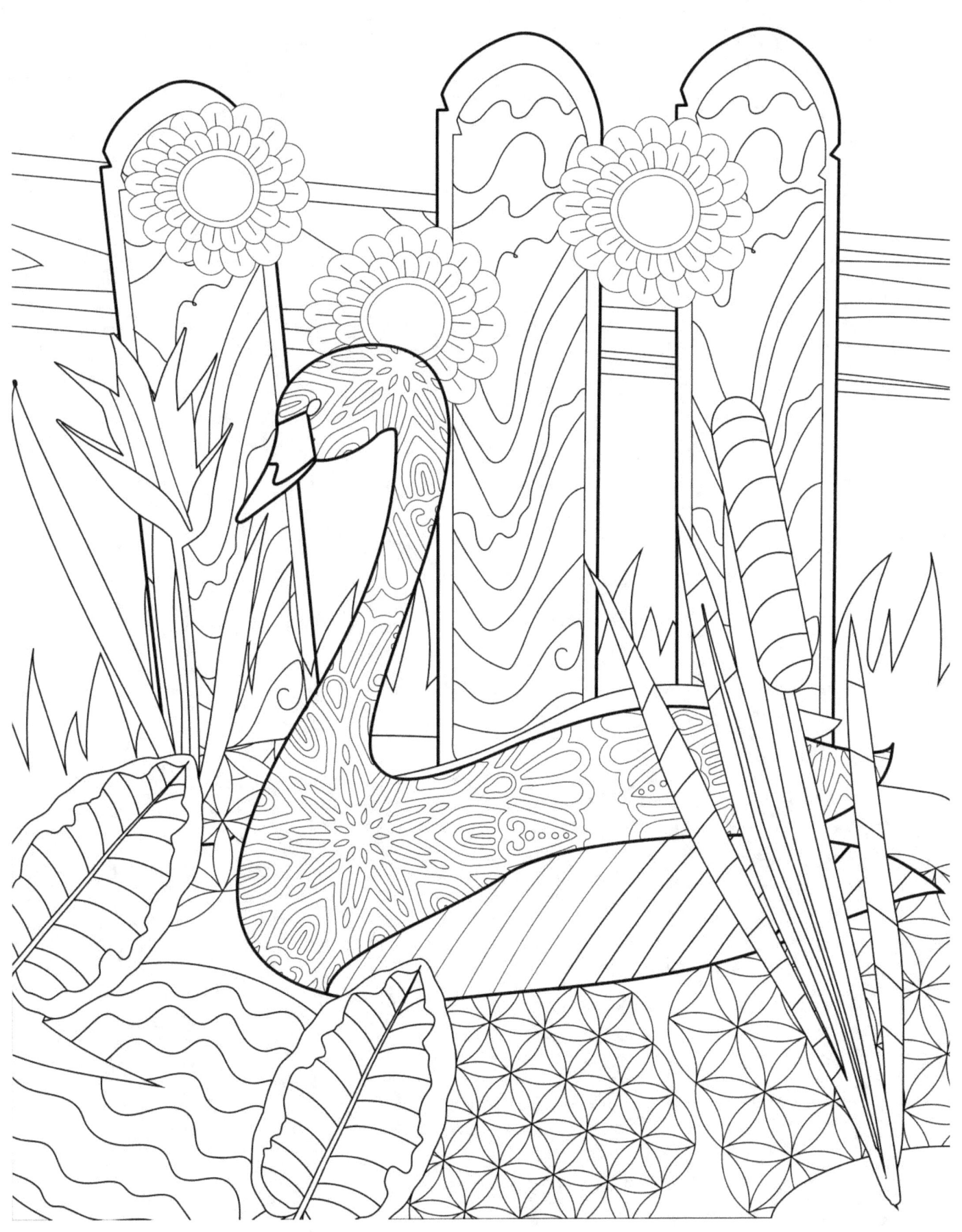

*Thank you for purchasing our Coloring Book!*
*Please leave us a review on Amazon.*

*Thank you for purchasing our Coloring Book!*

Thank you for purchasing our Coloring Book!
Please leave us a review on Amazon.

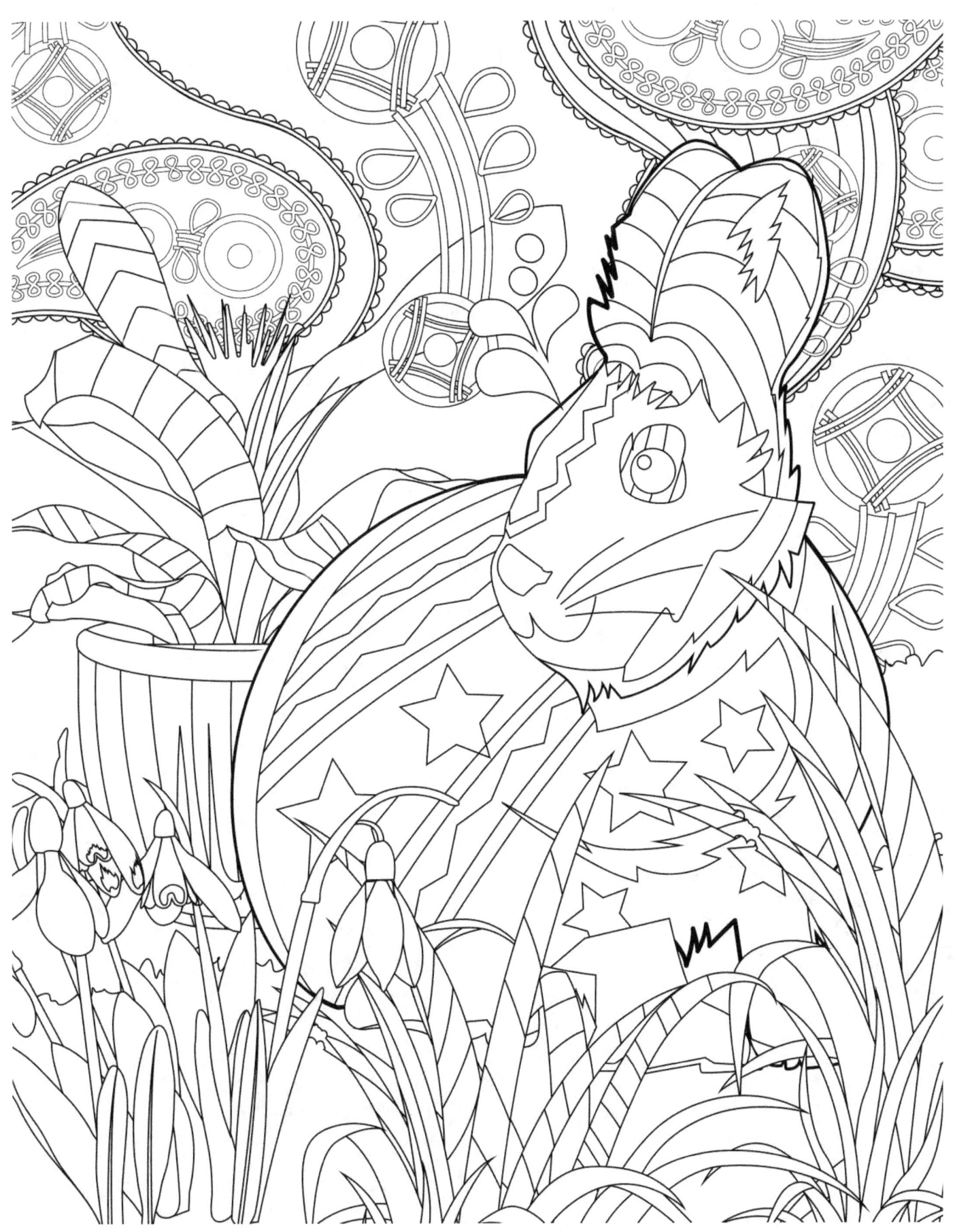

Thank you for purchasing our Coloring Book!
Please leave us a review on Amazon.

Thank you for purchasing our Coloring Book!
Please leave us a review on Amazon.

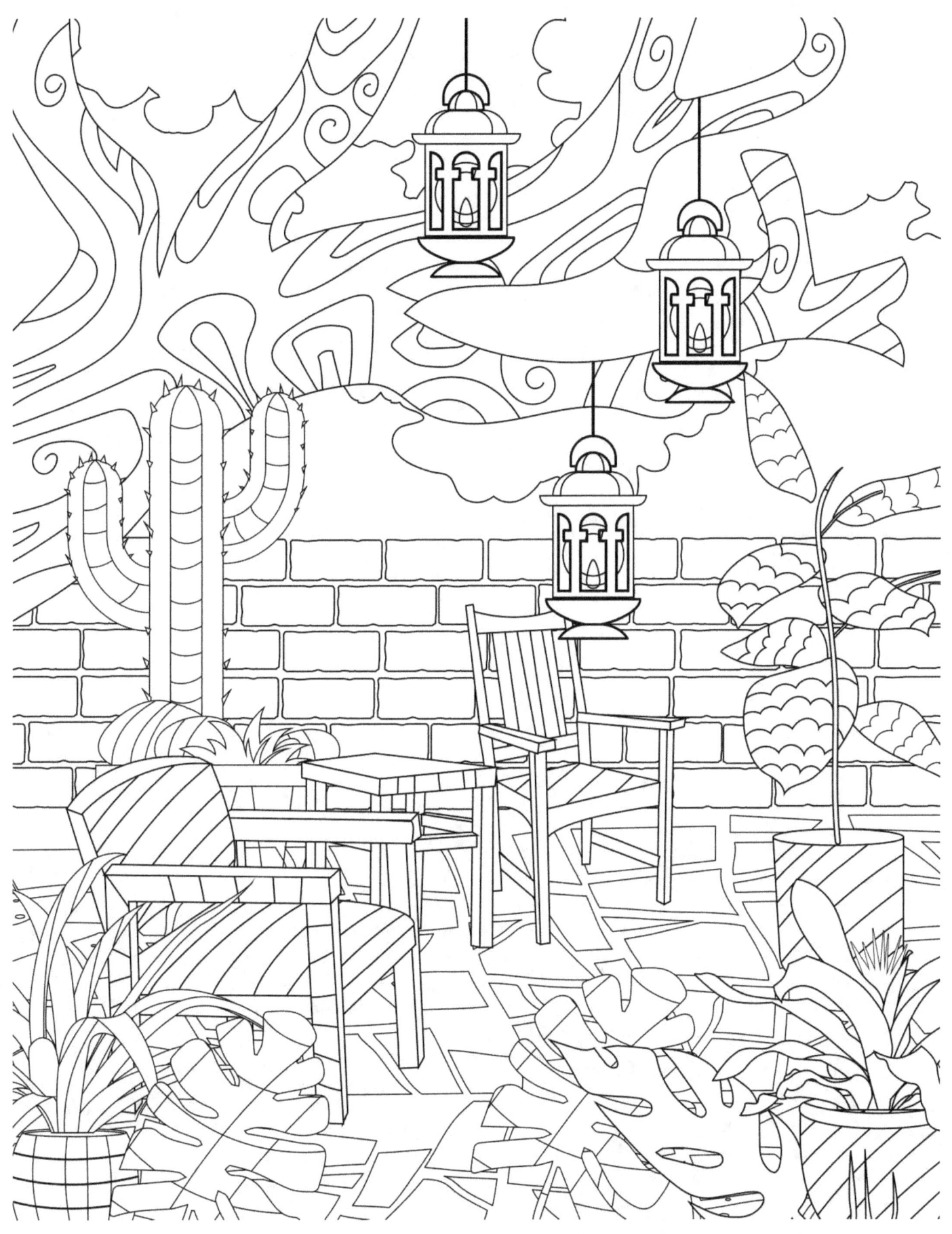

*Thank you for purchasing our Coloring Book!*
*Please leave us a review on Amazon.*

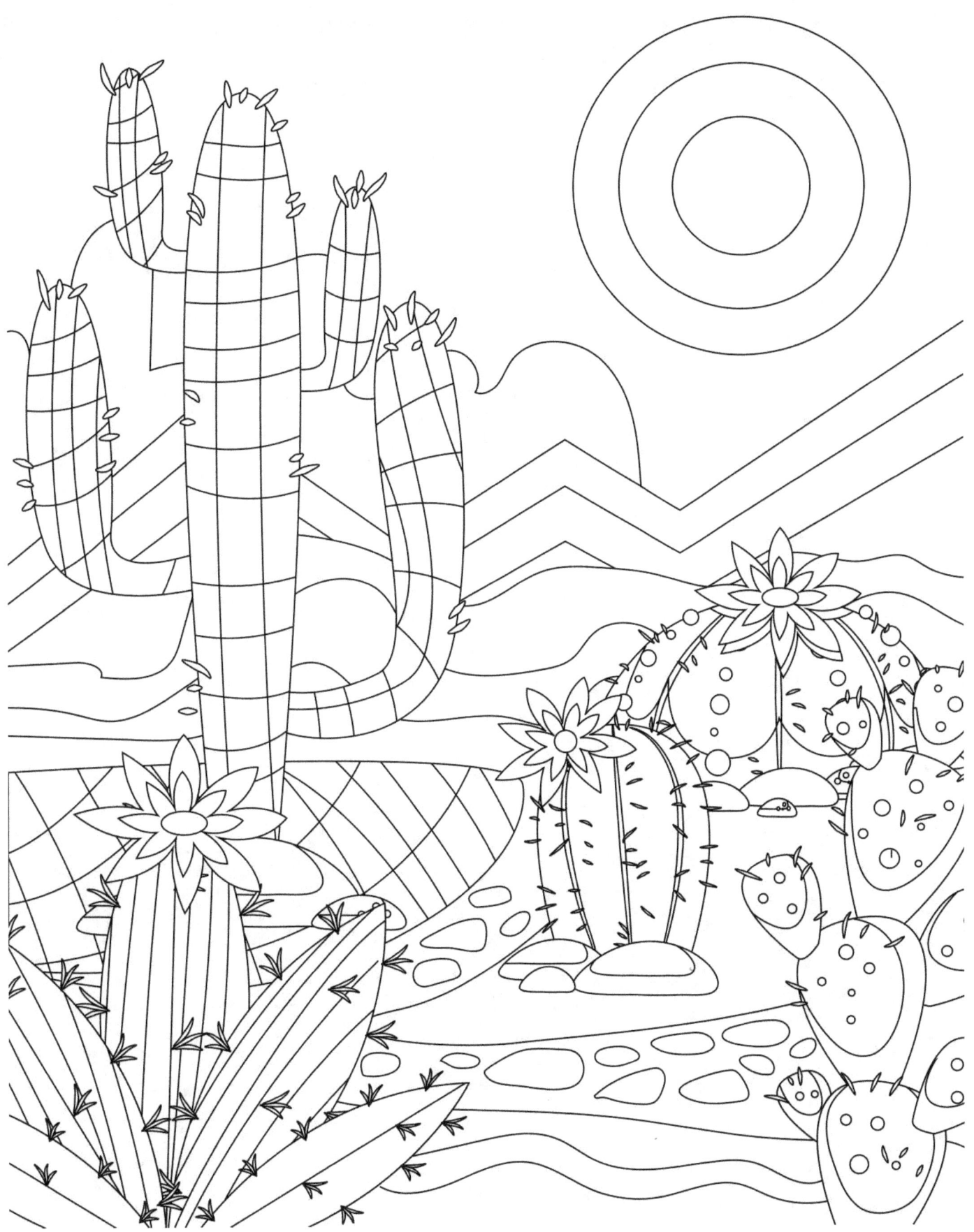

*Thank you for purchasing our Coloring Book!*
*Please leave us a review on Amazon.*

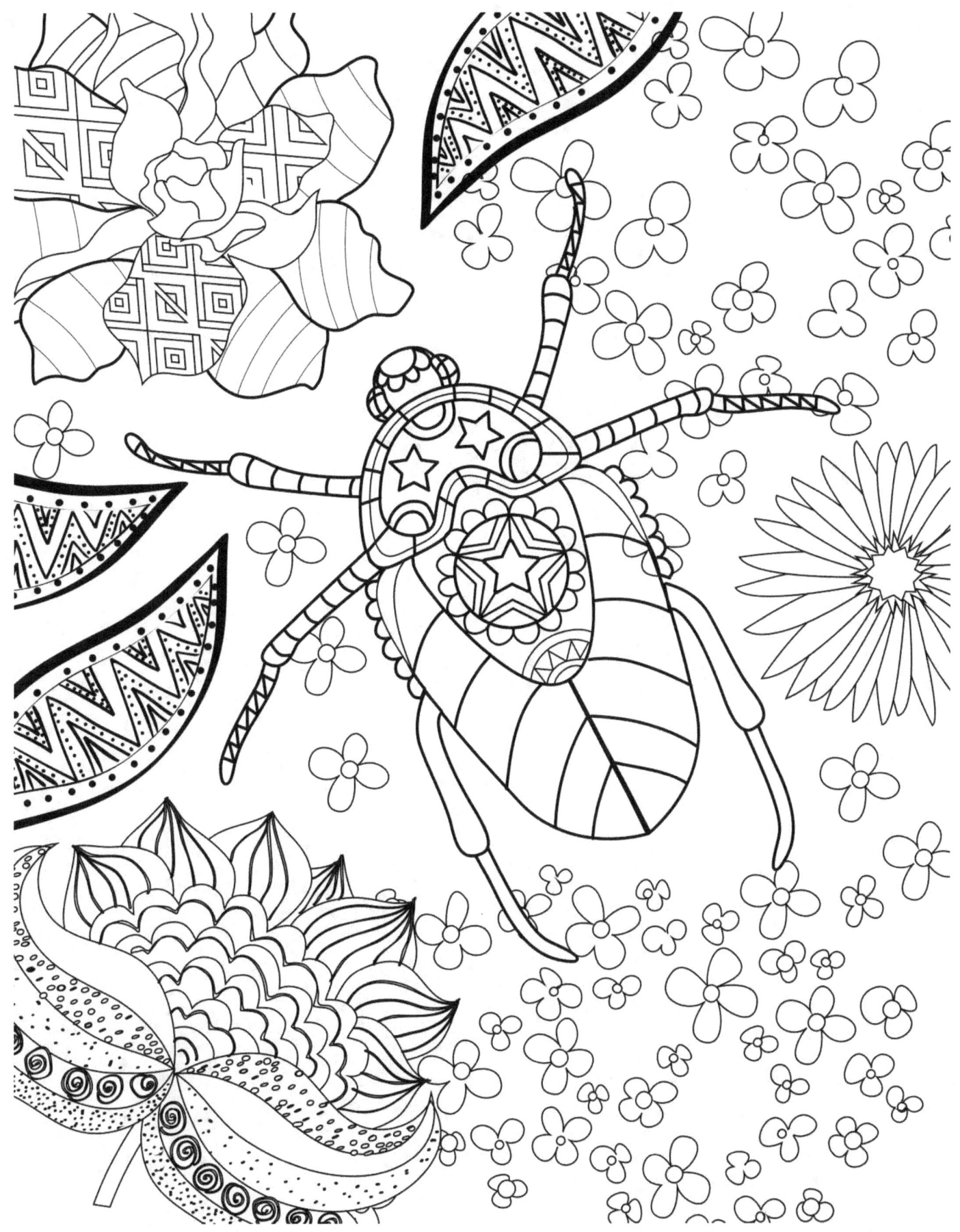

Thank you for purchasing our Coloring Book!
Please leave us a review on Amazon.

Thank you for purchasing our Coloring Book!

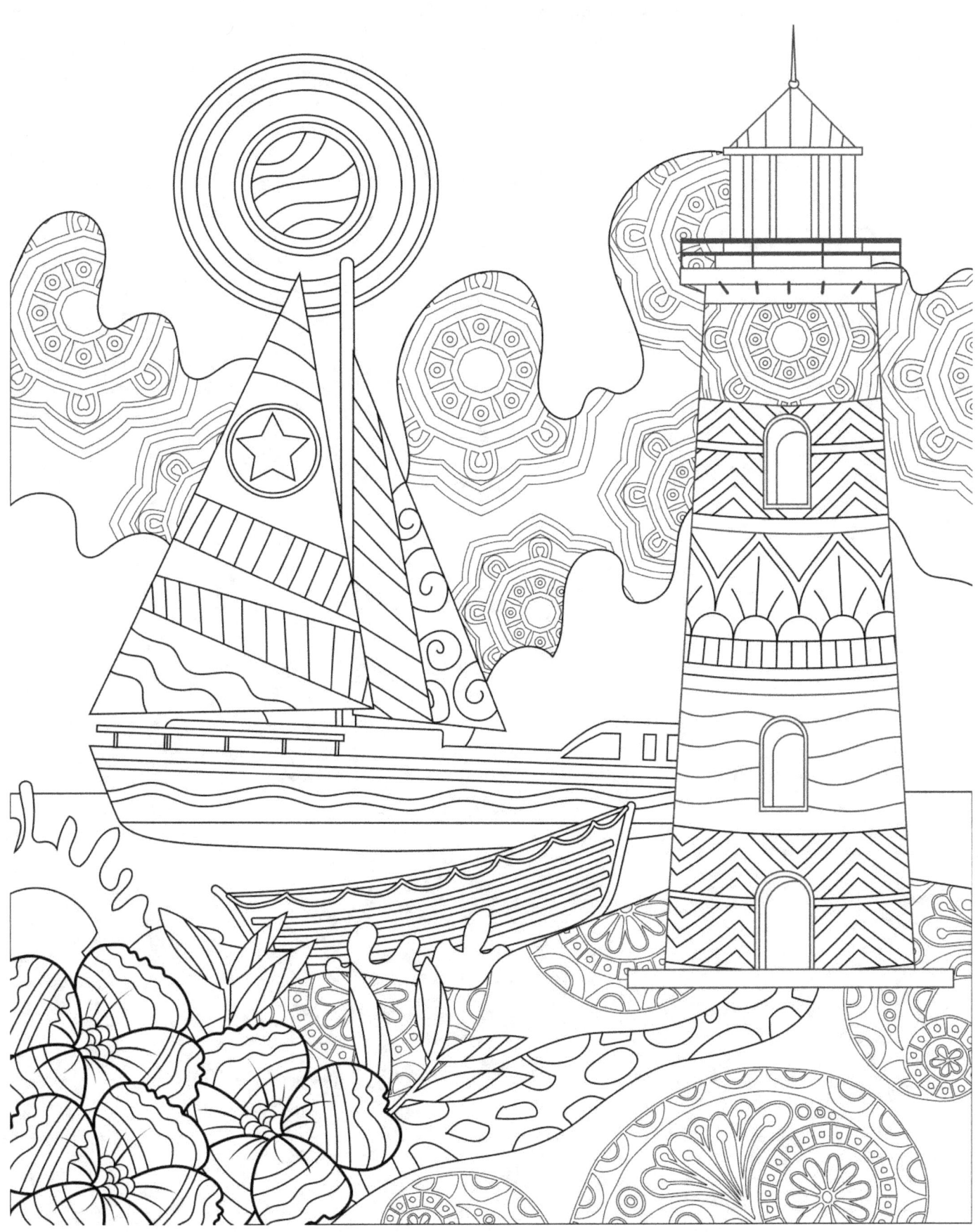

Thank you for purchasing our Coloring Book!
Please leave us a review on Amazon.

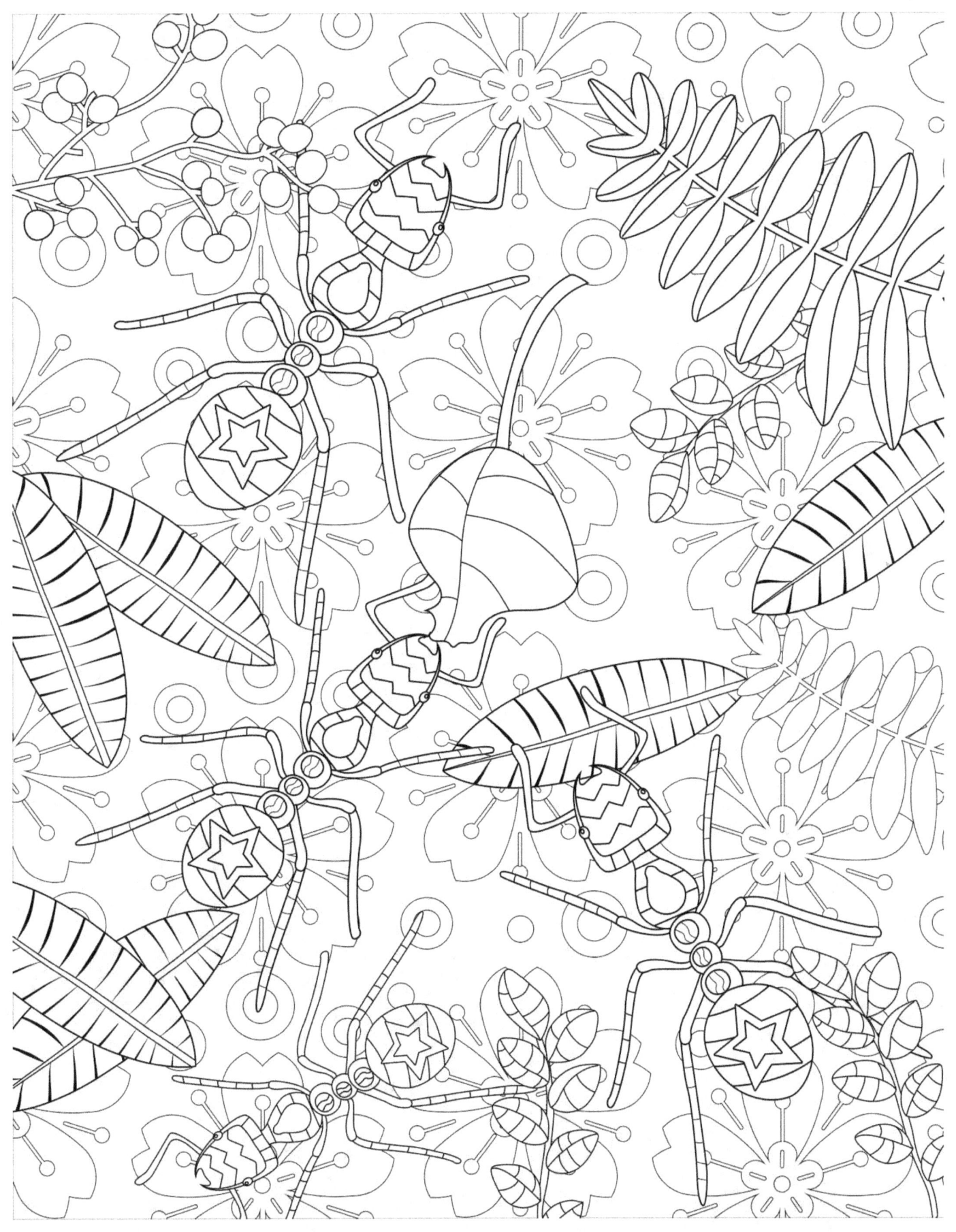

Thank you for purchasing our Coloring Book!
Please leave us a review on Amazon.

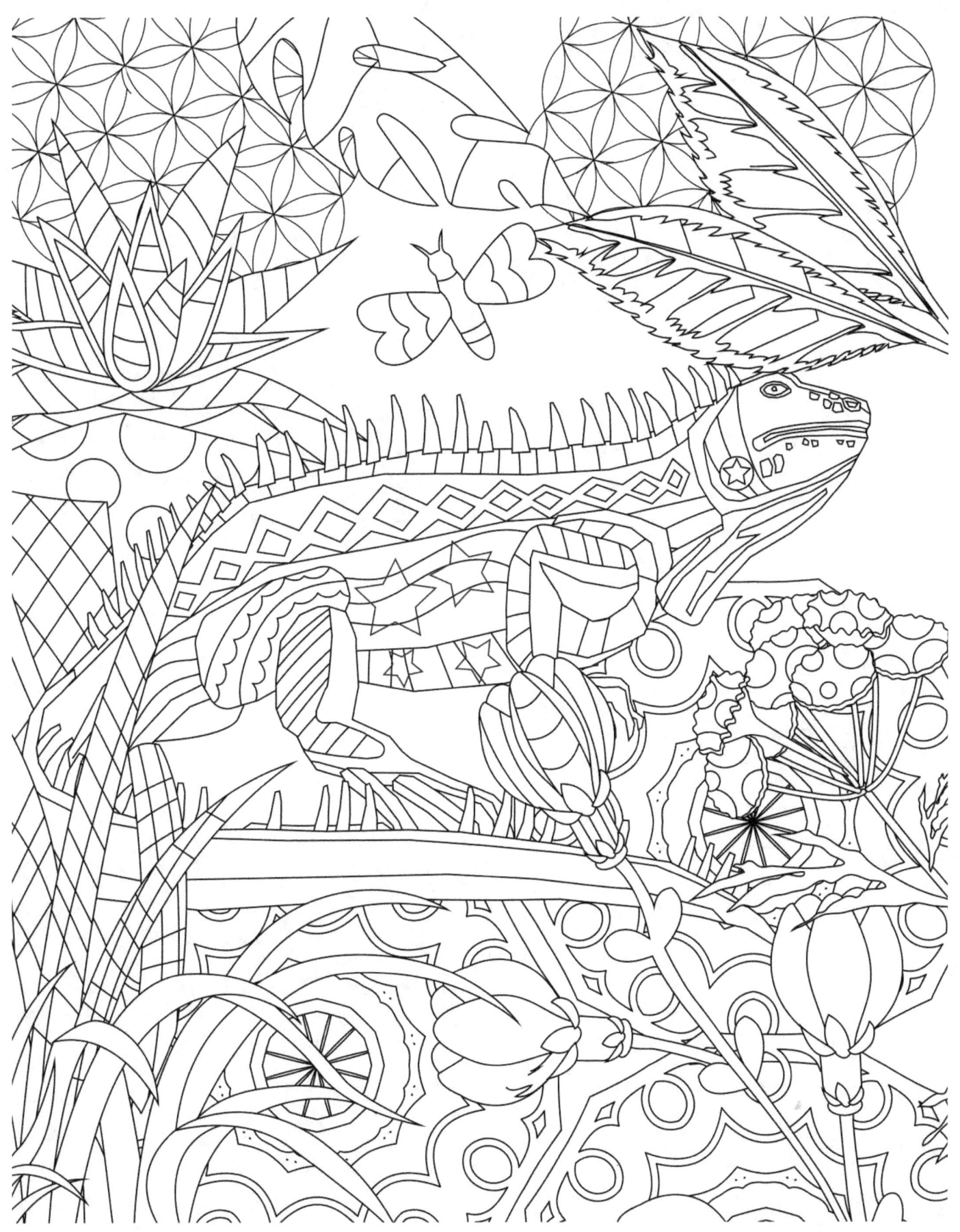

Thank you for purchasing our Coloring Book!
Please leave us a review on Amazon.

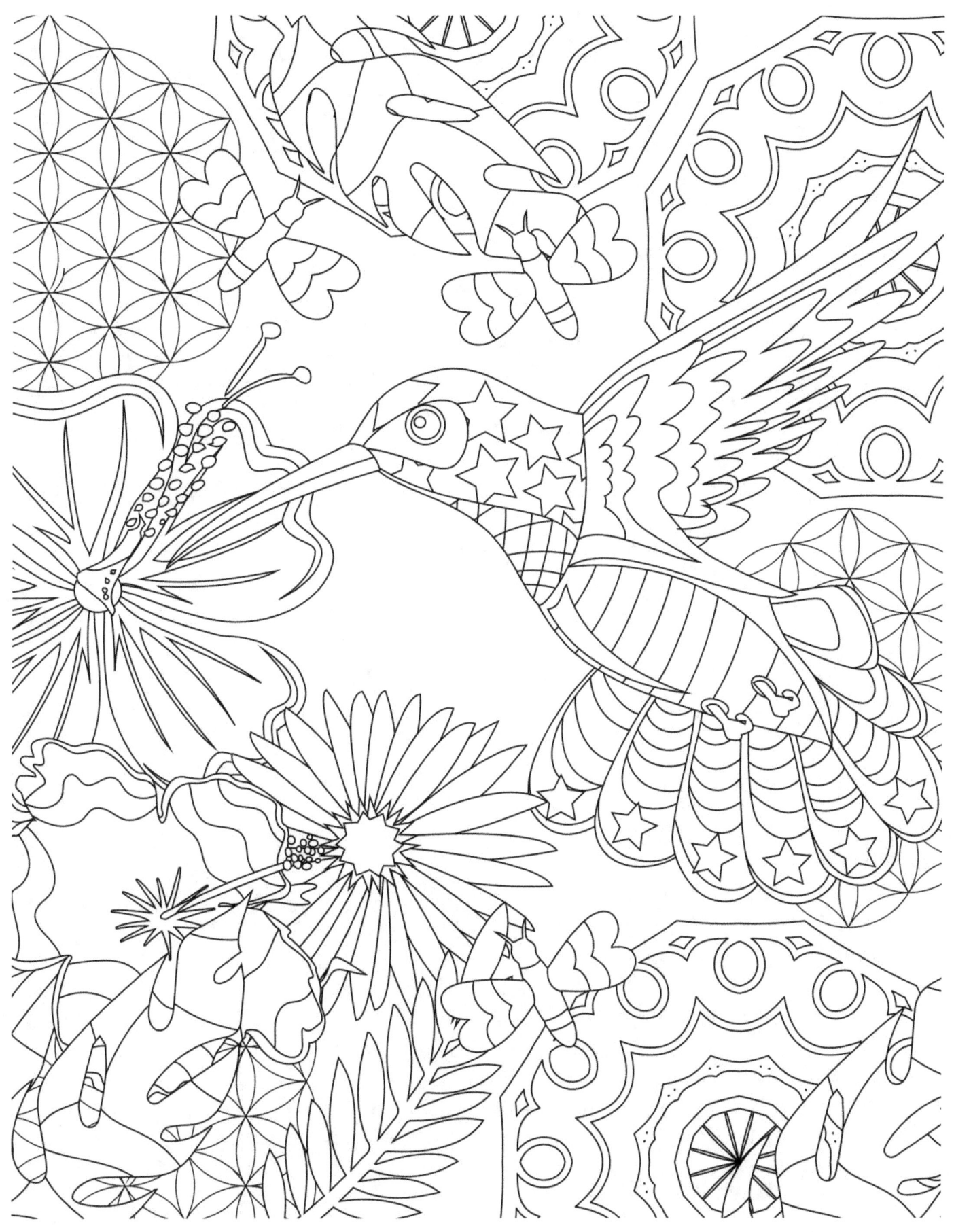

Thank you for purchasing our Coloring Book!
Please leave us a review on Amazon.

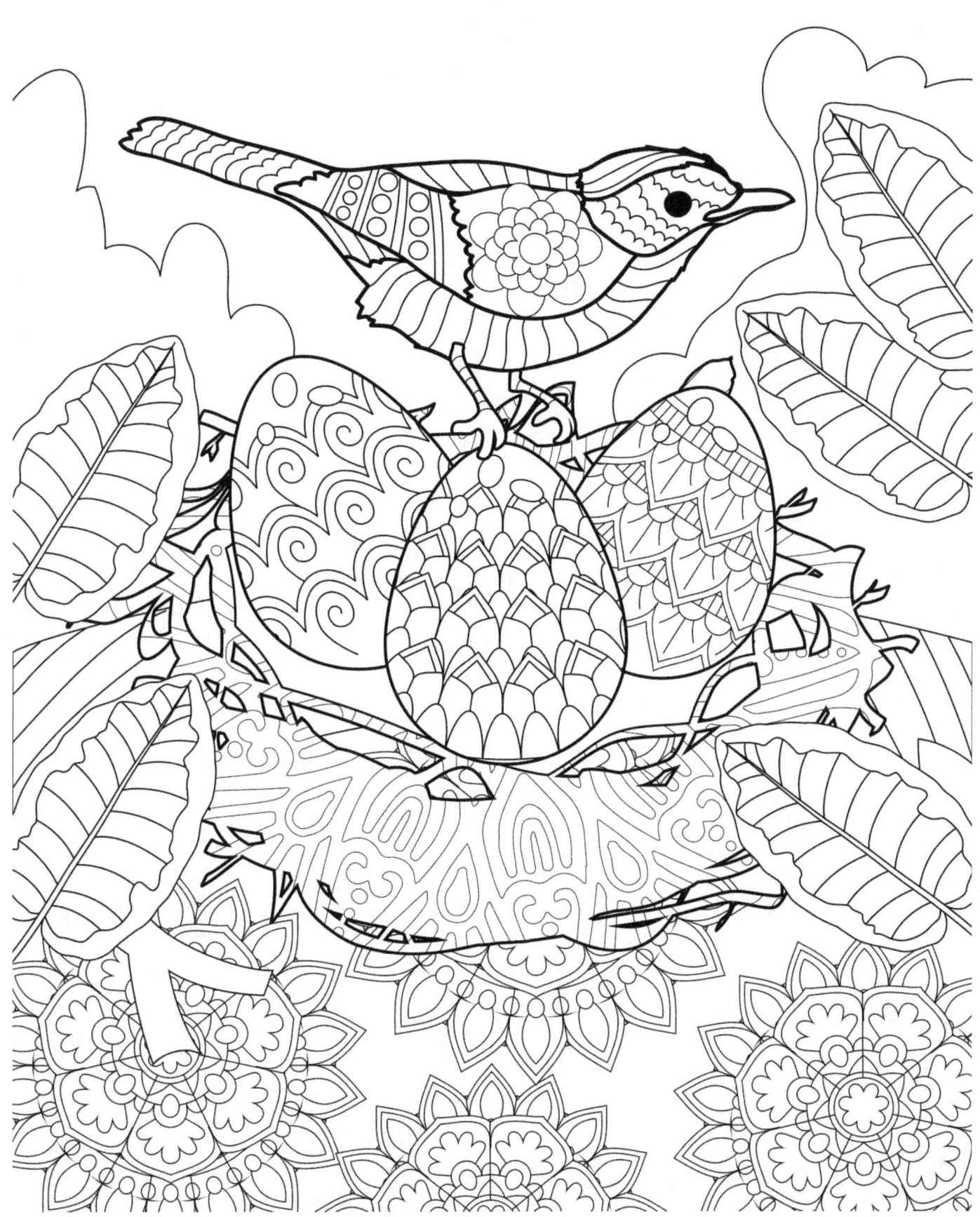

Thank you for purchasing our Coloring Book!
Please leave us a review on Amazon.

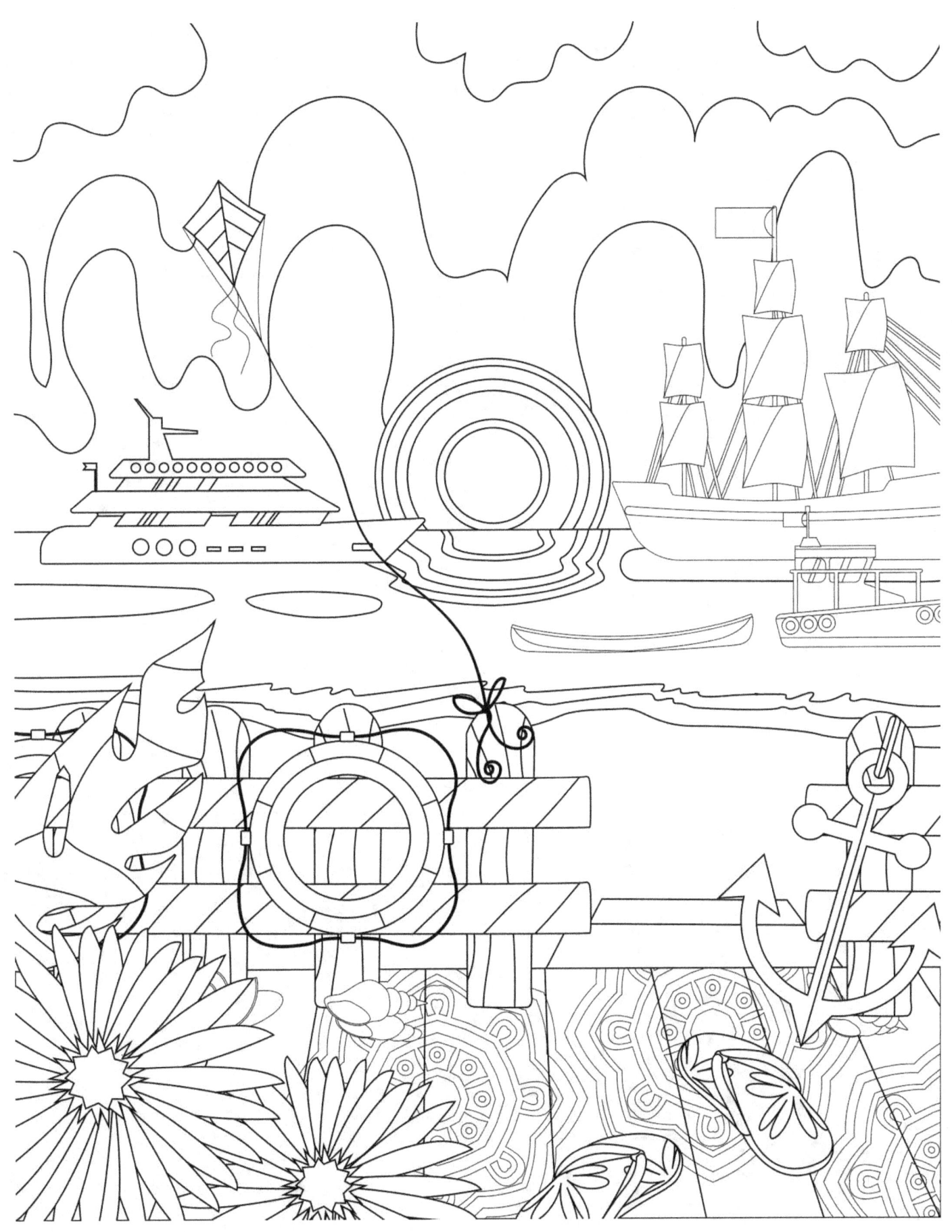

*Thank you for purchasing our Coloring Book!*
*Please leave us a review on Amazon.*

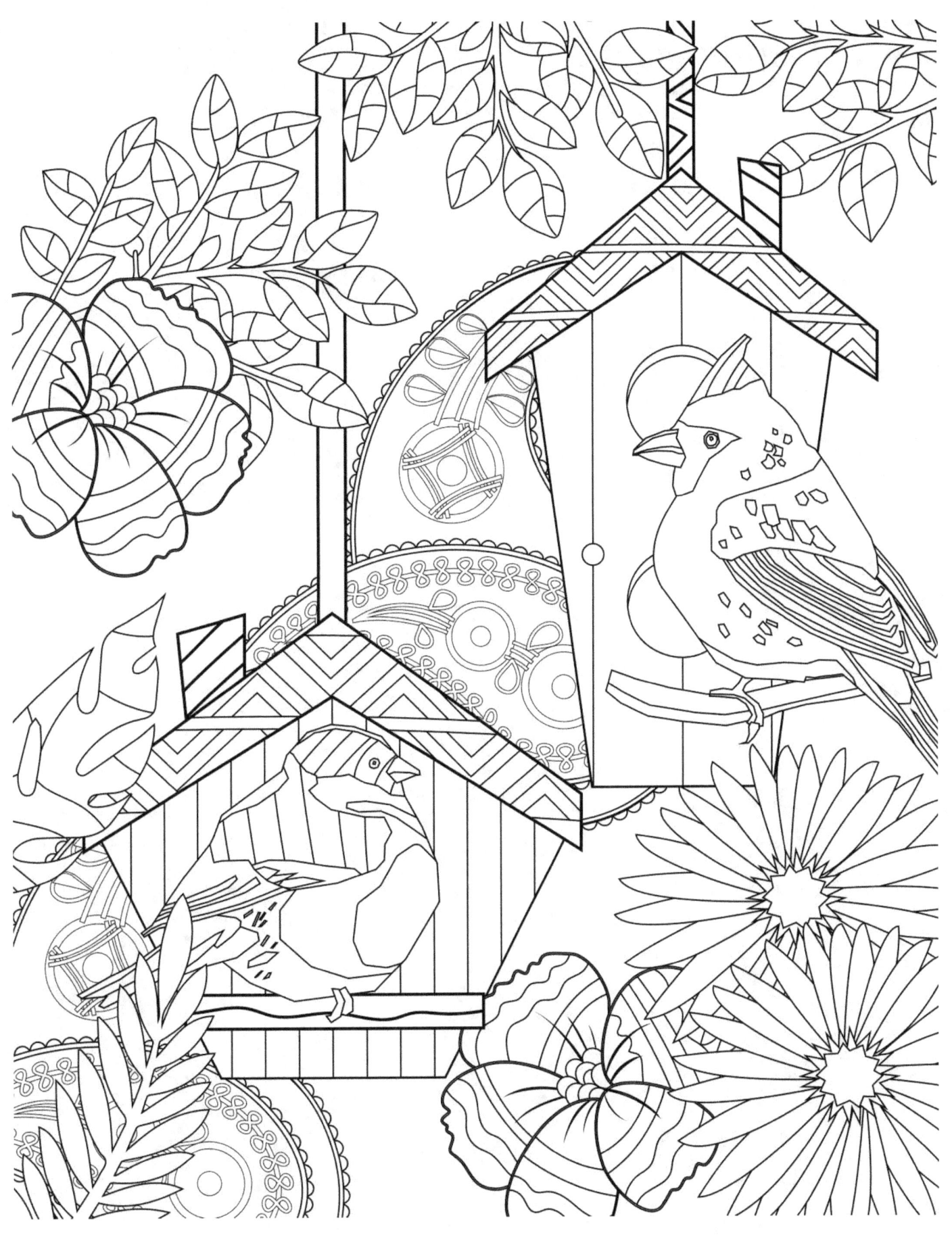

Thank you for purchasing our Coloring Book!
Please leave us a review on Amazon.

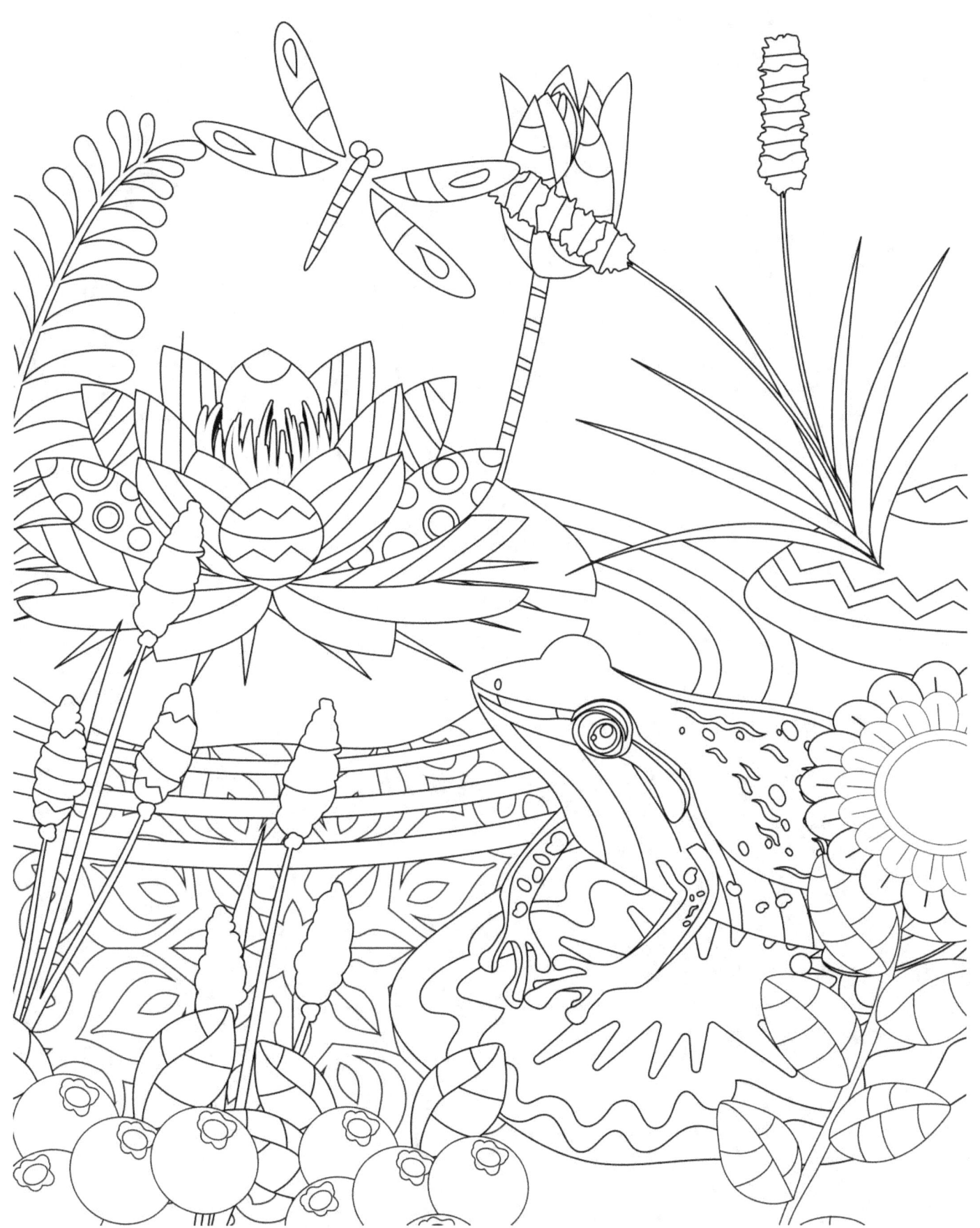

Thank you for purchasing our Coloring Book!
Please leave us a review on Amazon.

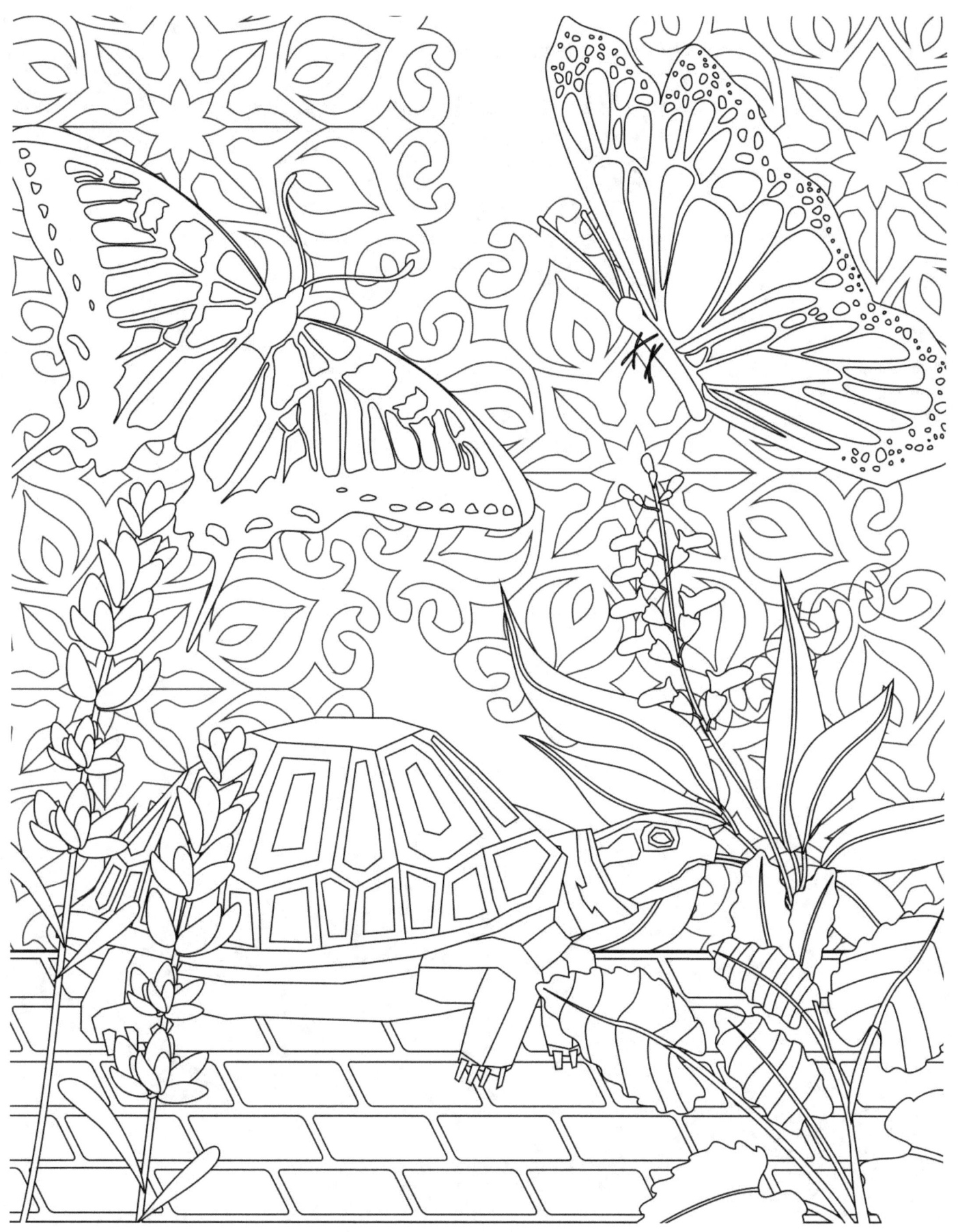

Thank you for purchasing our Coloring Book!
Please leave us a review on Amazon.

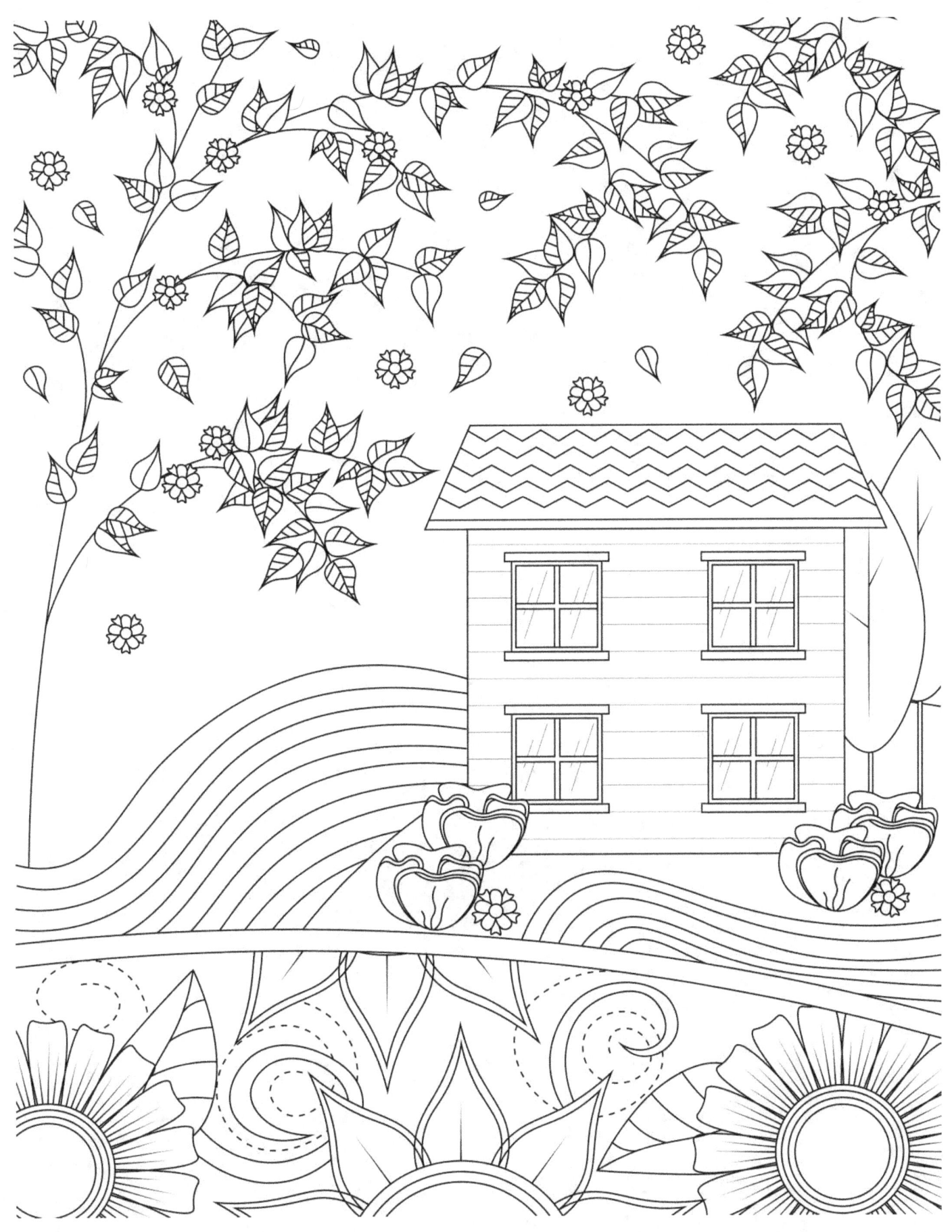

Thank you for purchasing our Coloring Book!
Please leave us a review on Amazon.

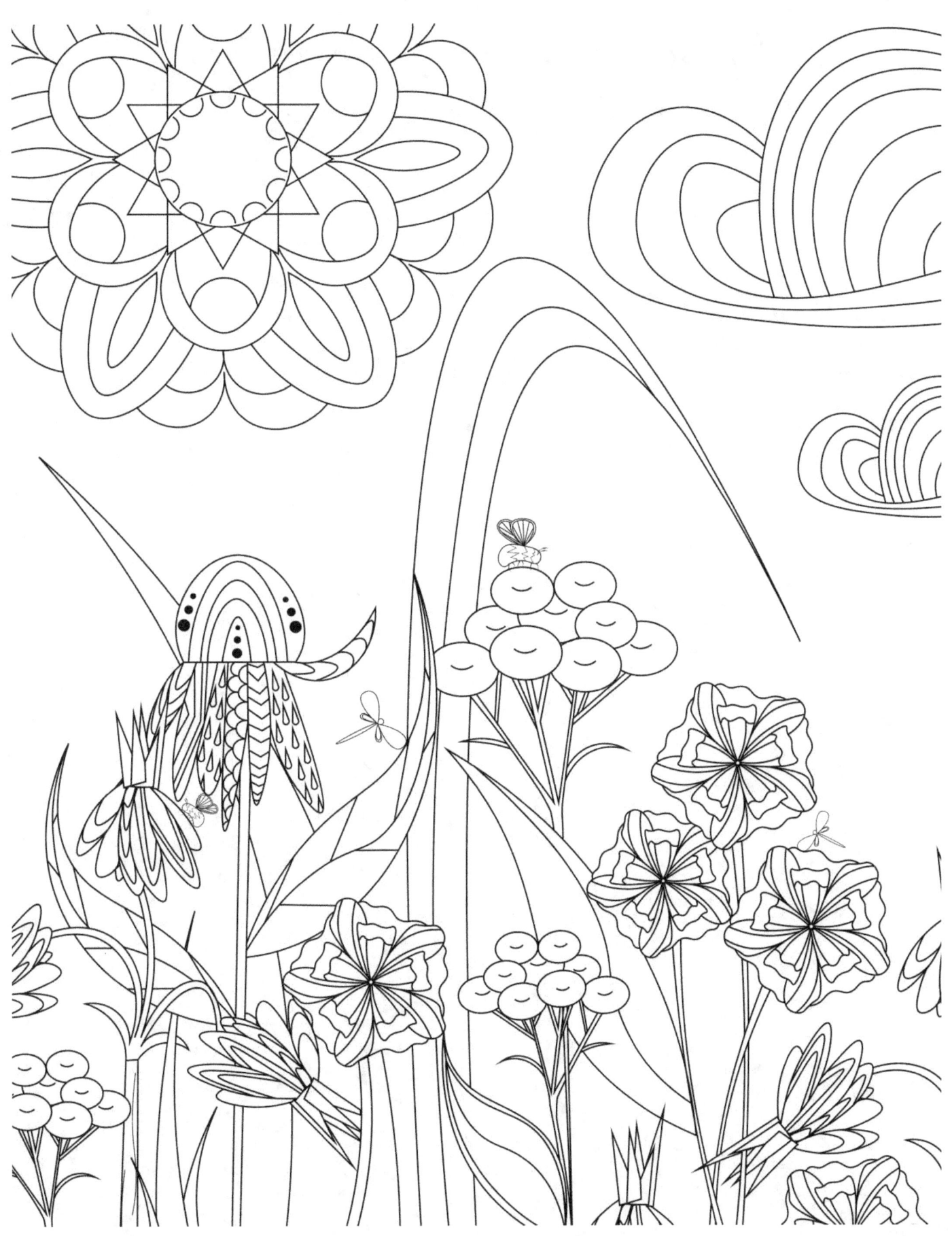

Thank you for purchasing our Coloring Book!
Please leave us a review on Amazon.

Thank you for purchasing our Coloring Book!

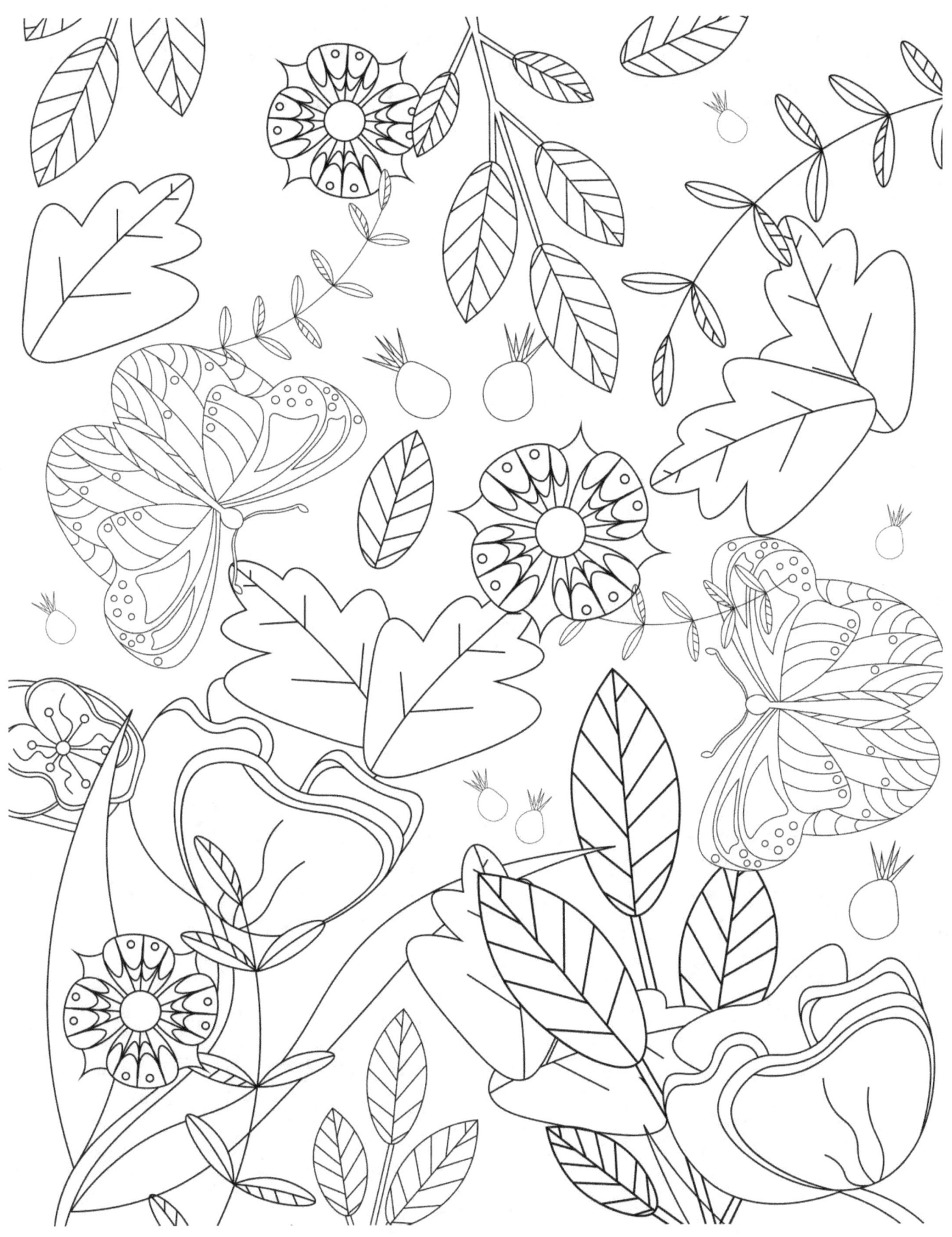

Thank you for purchasing our Coloring Book!
Please leave us a review on Amazon.

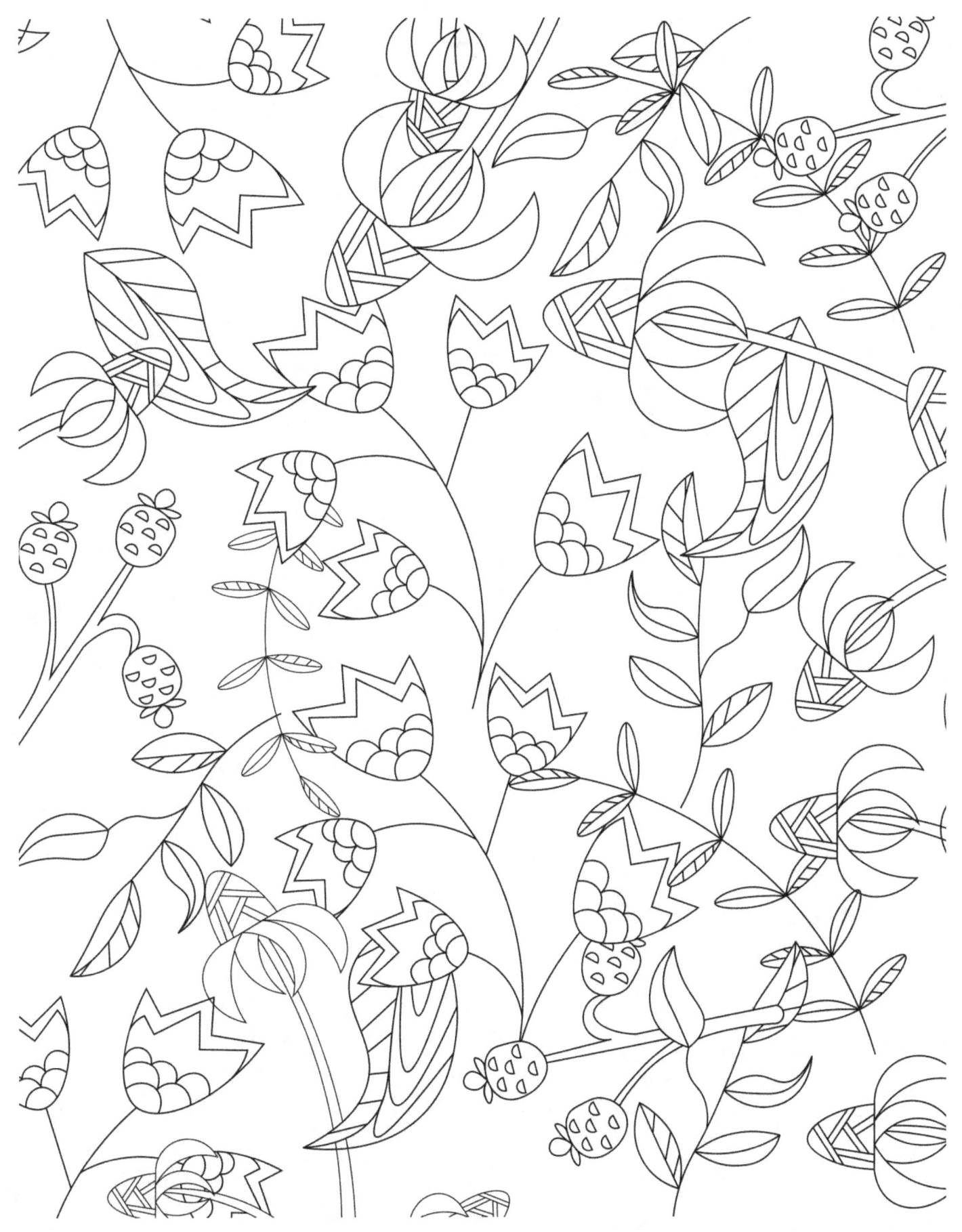

Thank you for purchasing our Coloring Book!
Please leave us a review on Amazon.

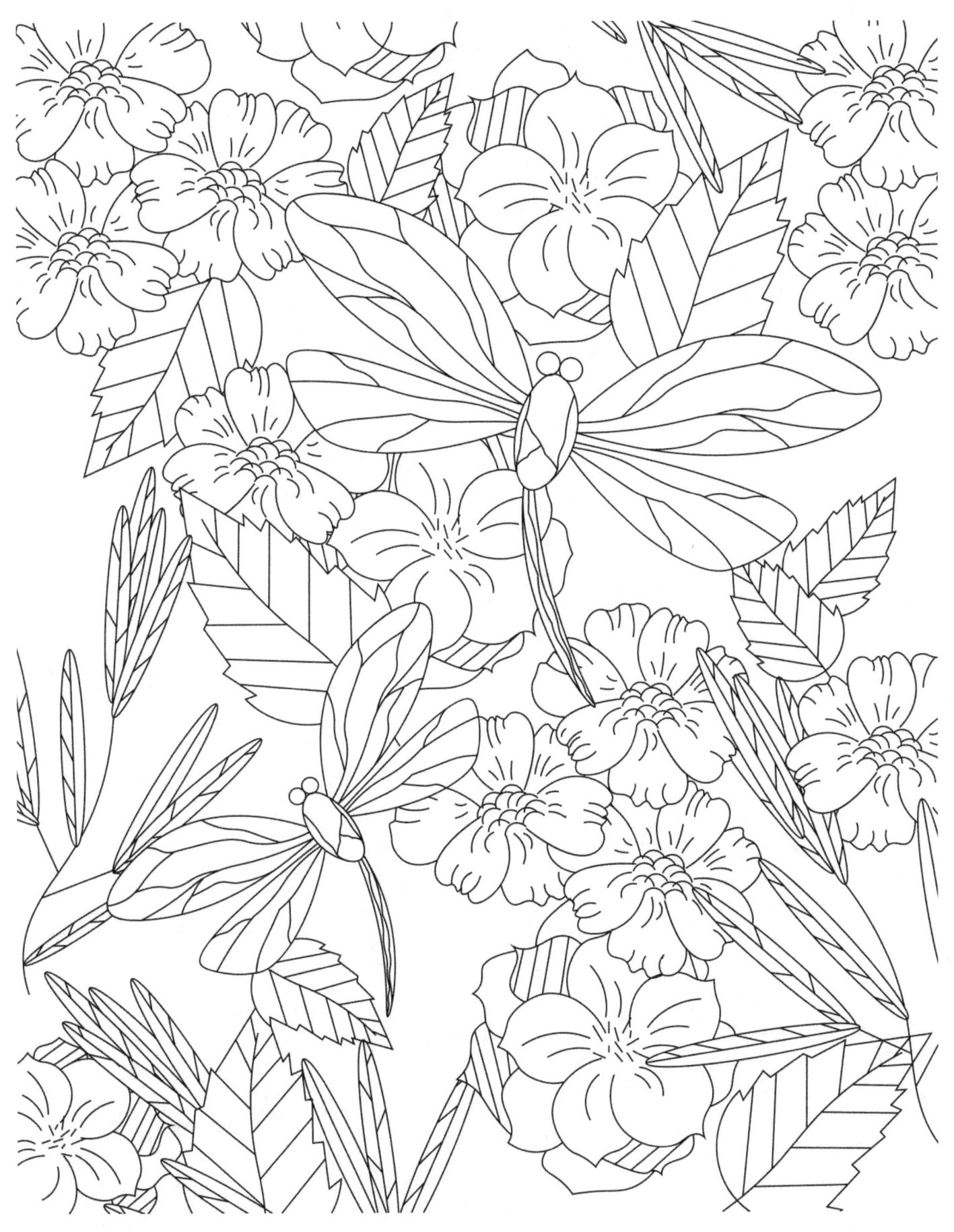

Thank you for purchasing our Coloring Book!
Please leave us a review on Amazon.

Thank you for purchasing our Coloring Book!
Please leave us a review on Amazon.

Thank you for purchasing our Coloring Book!
Please leave us a review on Amazon.

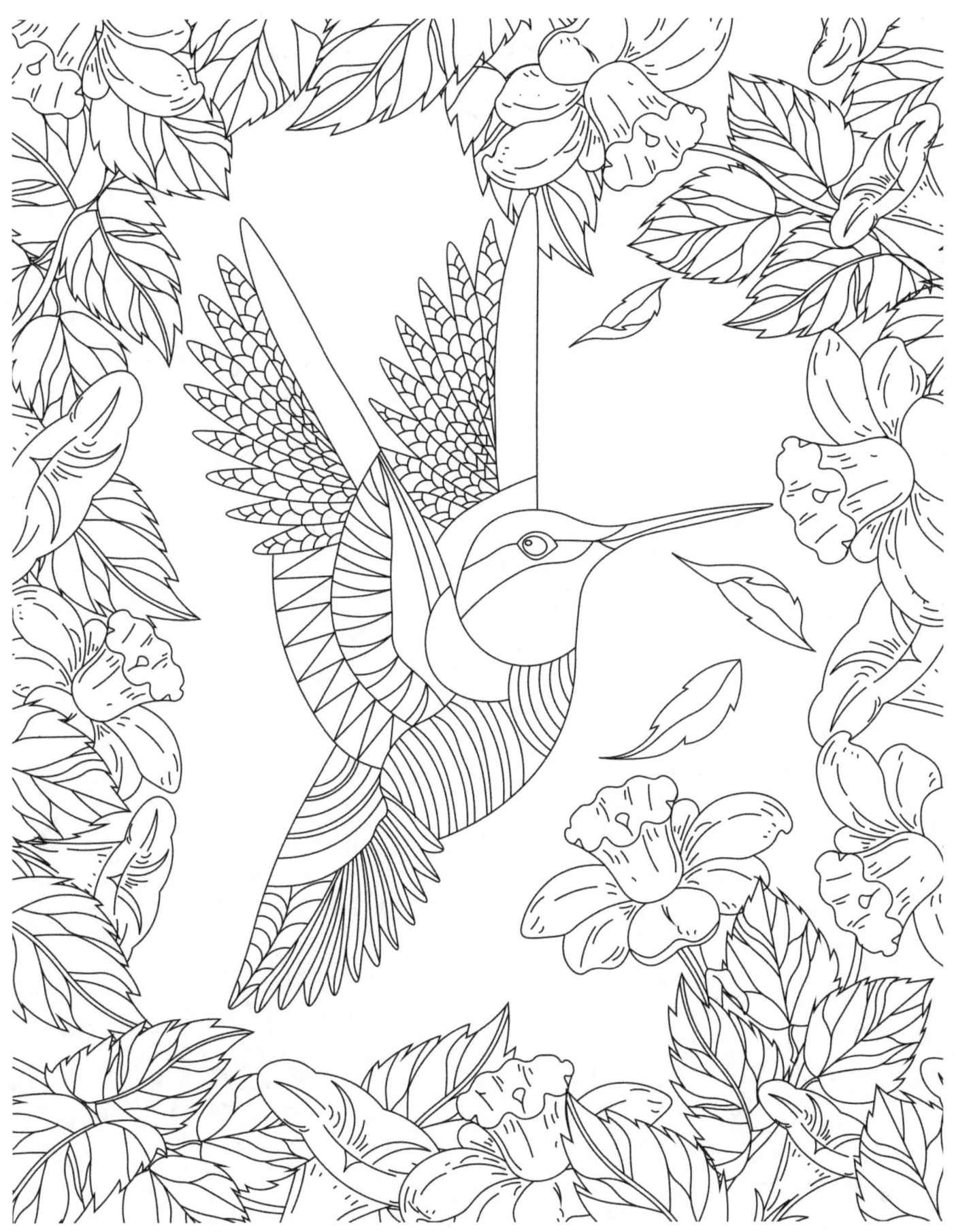

Thank you for purchasing our Coloring Book!
Please leave us a review on Amazon.

Thank you for purchasing our Coloring Book!
Please leave us a review on Amazon.

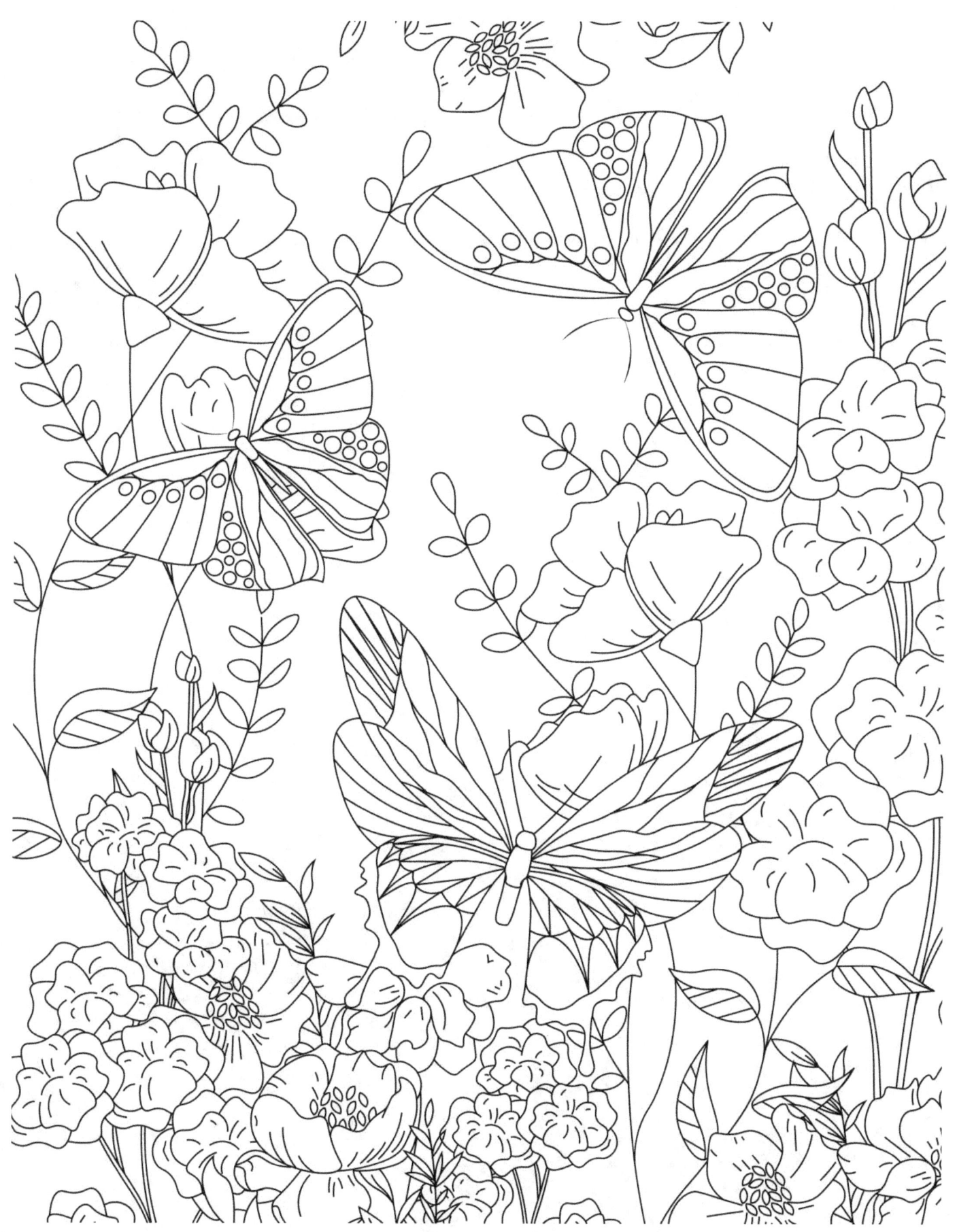

Thank you for purchasing our Coloring Book!
Please leave us a review on Amazon.

*Thank you for purchasing our Coloring Book!*
*Please leave us a review on Amazon.*

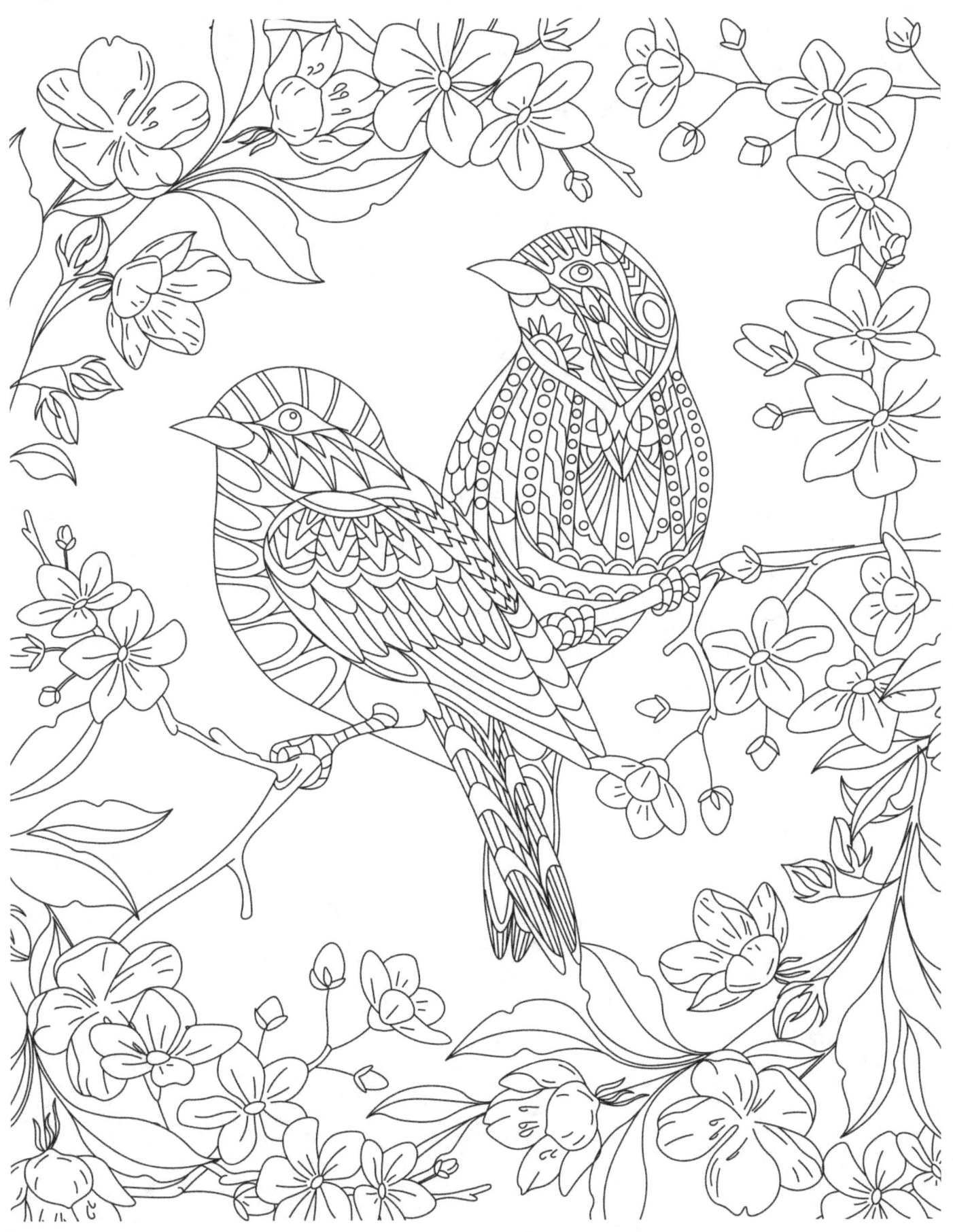

Thank you for purchasing our Coloring Book!
Please leave us a review on Amazon.

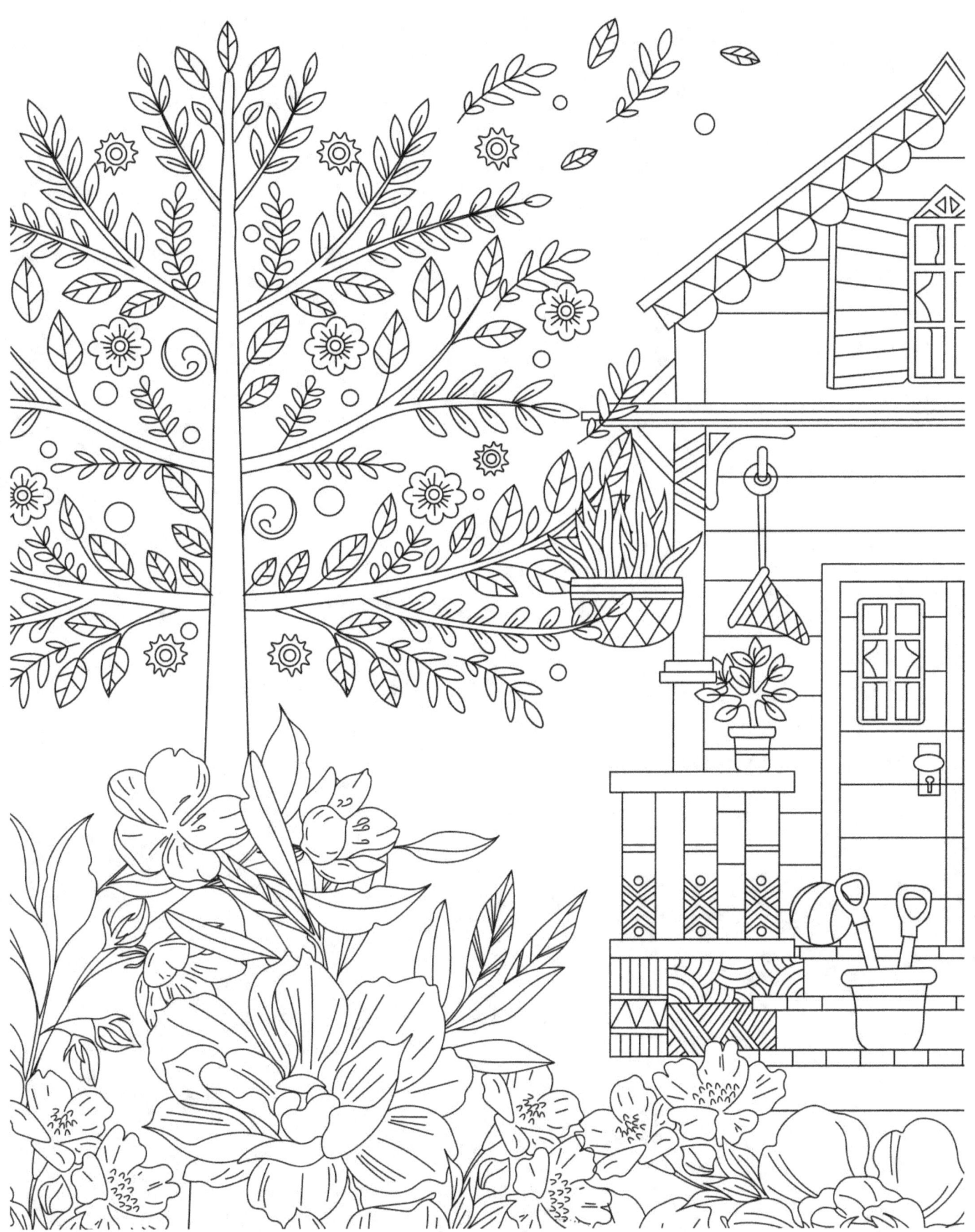

Thank you for purchasing our Coloring Book!
Please leave us a review on Amazon.

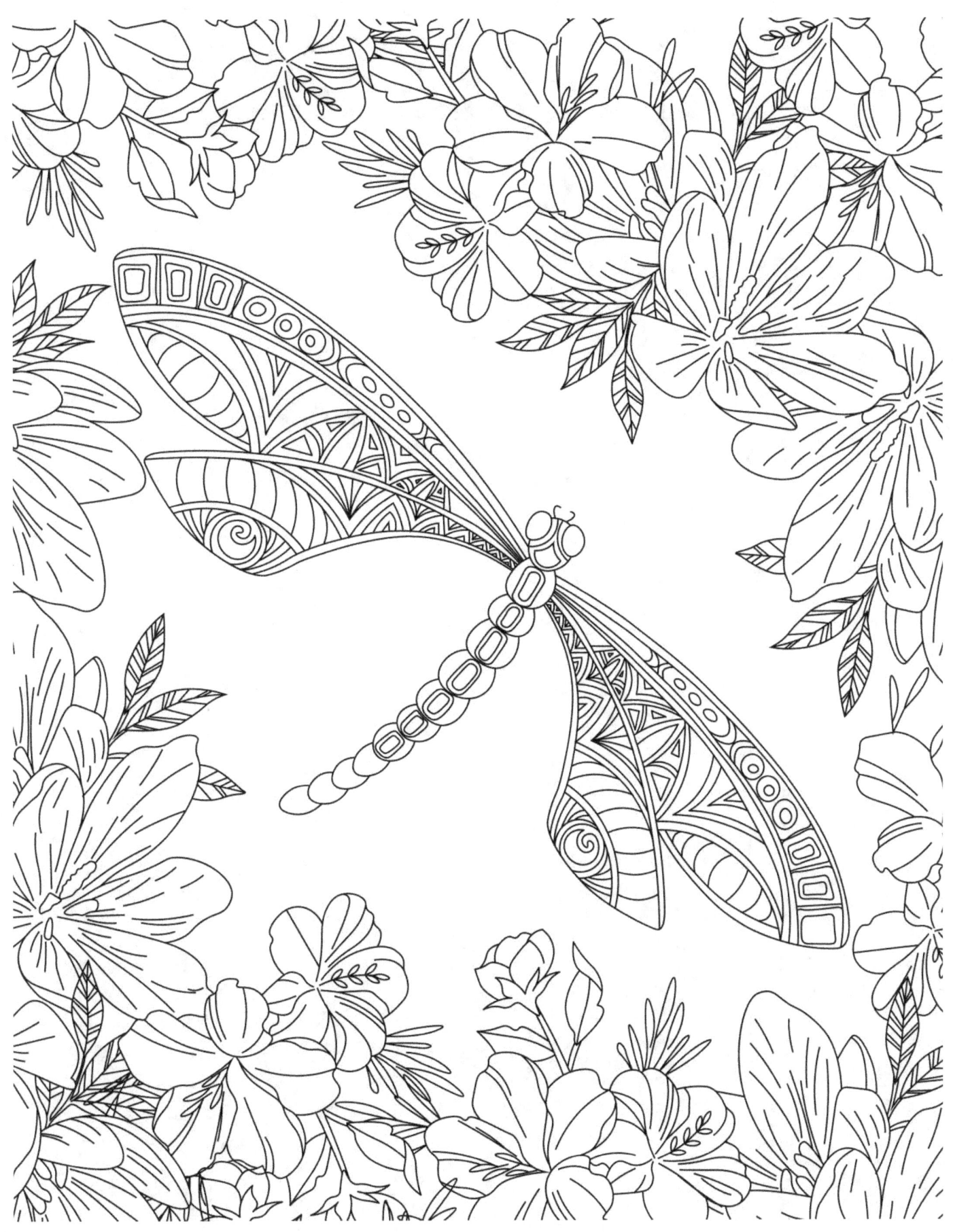

Thank you for purchasing our Coloring Book!
Please leave us a review on Amazon.

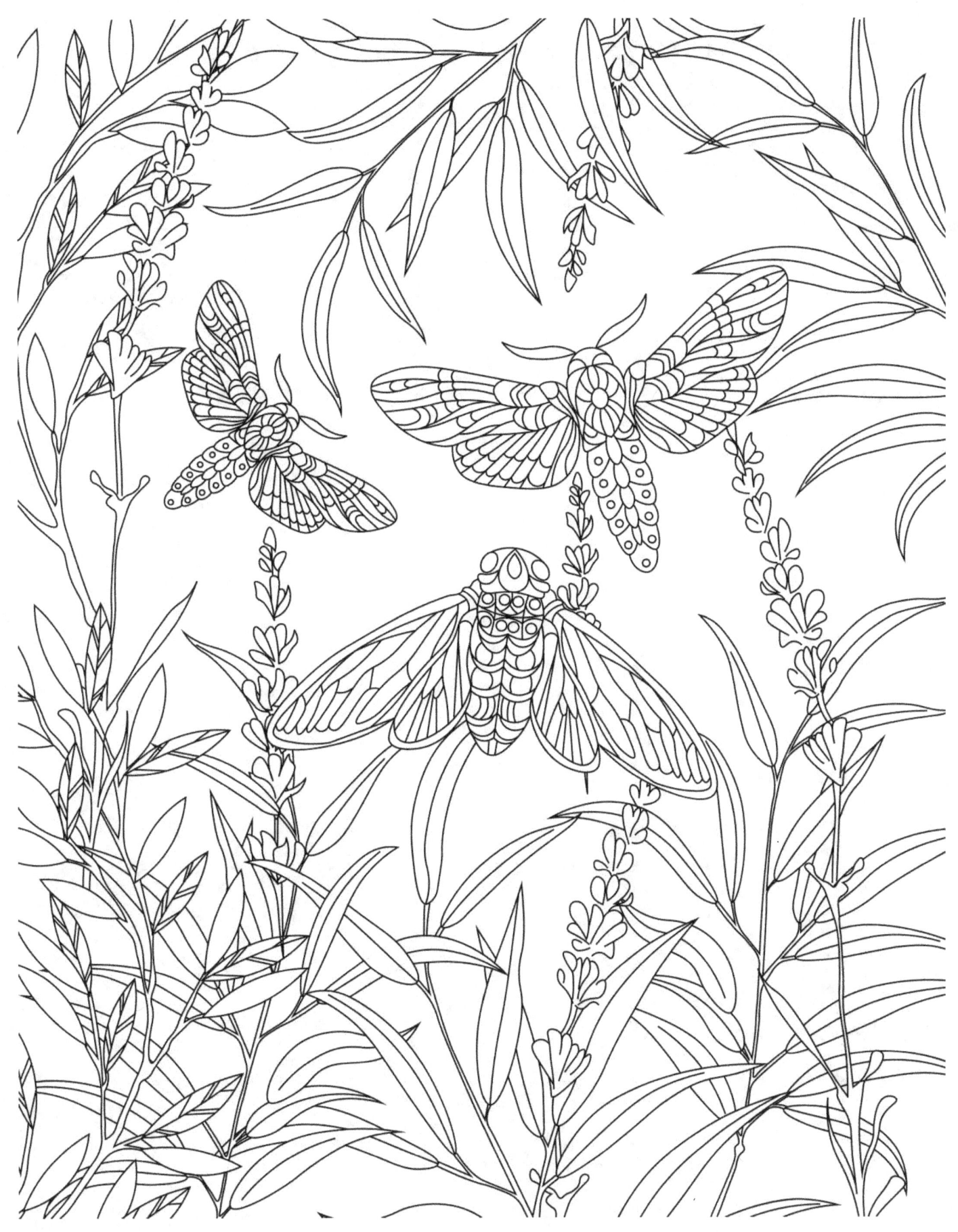

Thank you for purchasing our Coloring Book!
Please leave us a review on Amazon.

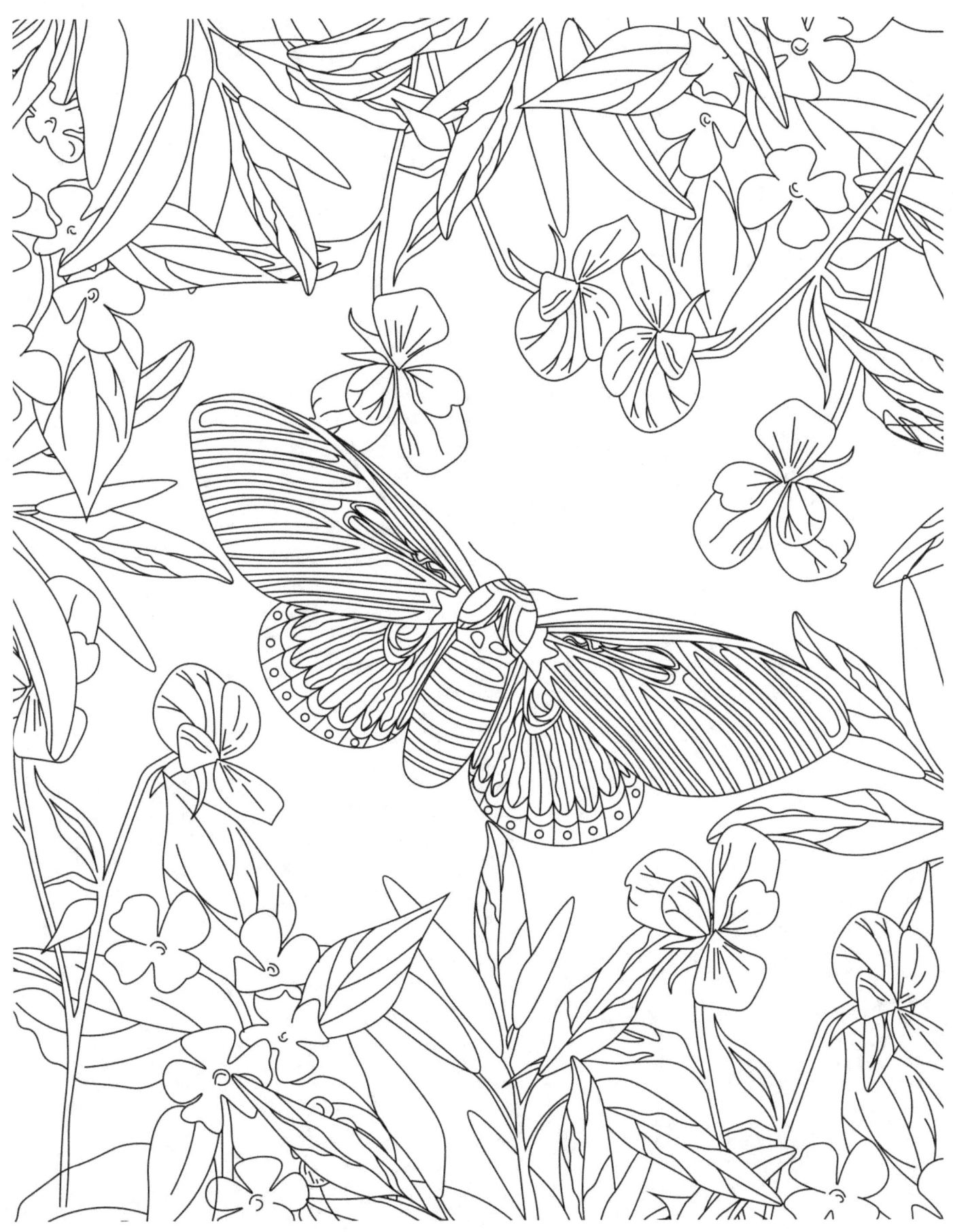

Thank you for purchasing our Coloring Book!
Please leave us a review on Amazon.

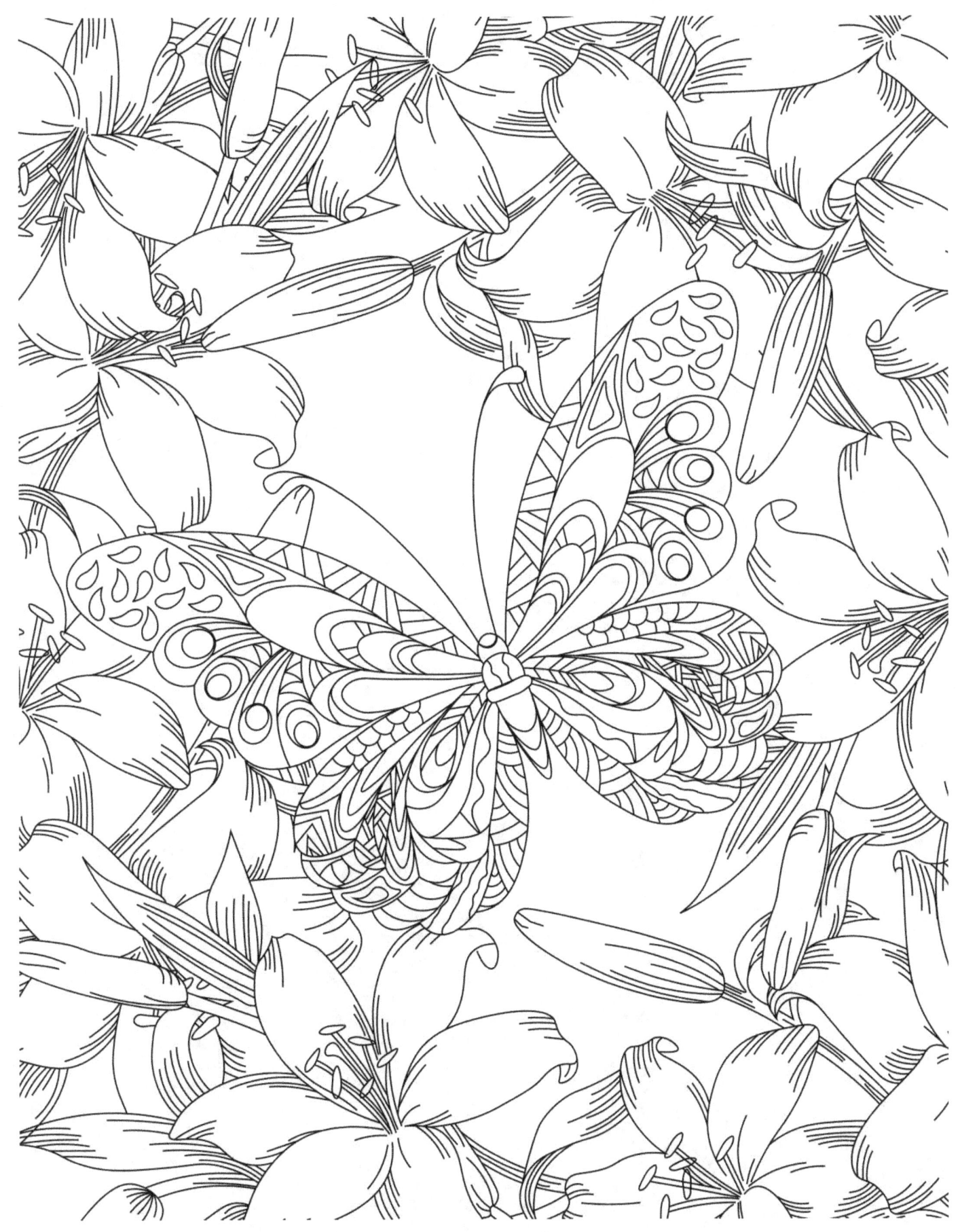

Thank you for purchasing our Coloring Book!
Please leave us a review on Amazon.

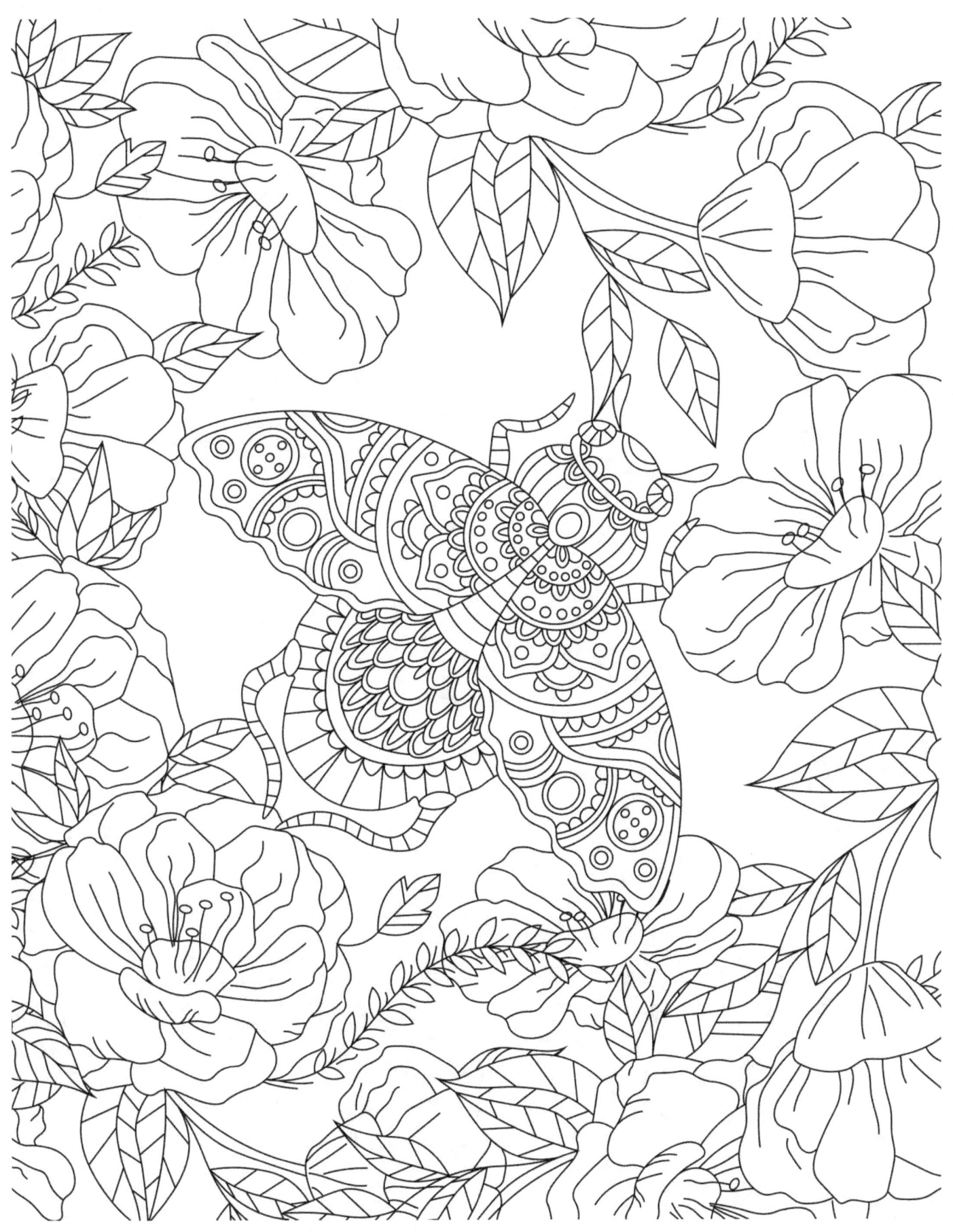

Thank you for purchasing our Coloring Book!
Please leave us a review on Amazon.

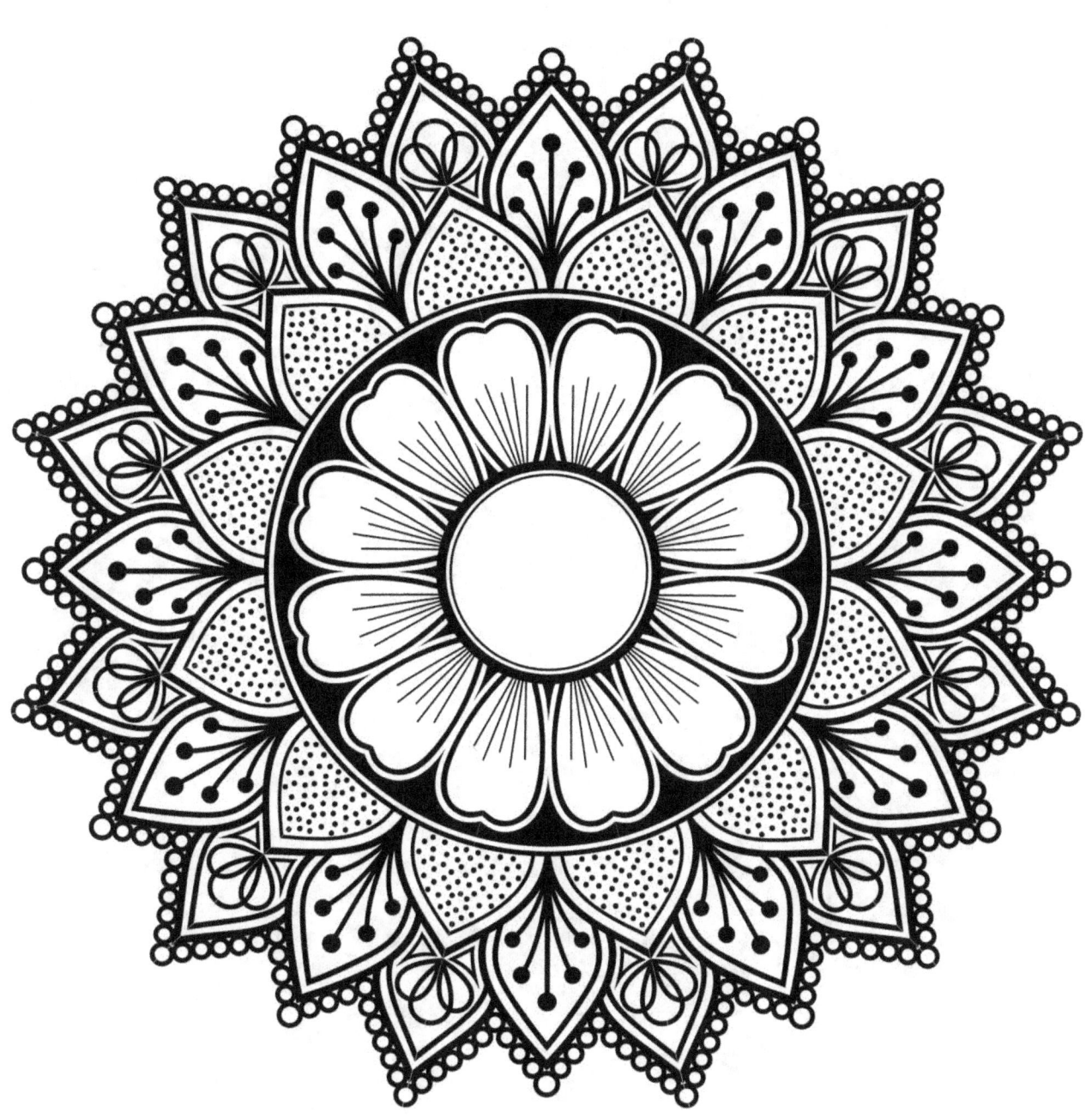

Thank you for purchasing our Coloring Book!
Please leave us a review on Amazon.

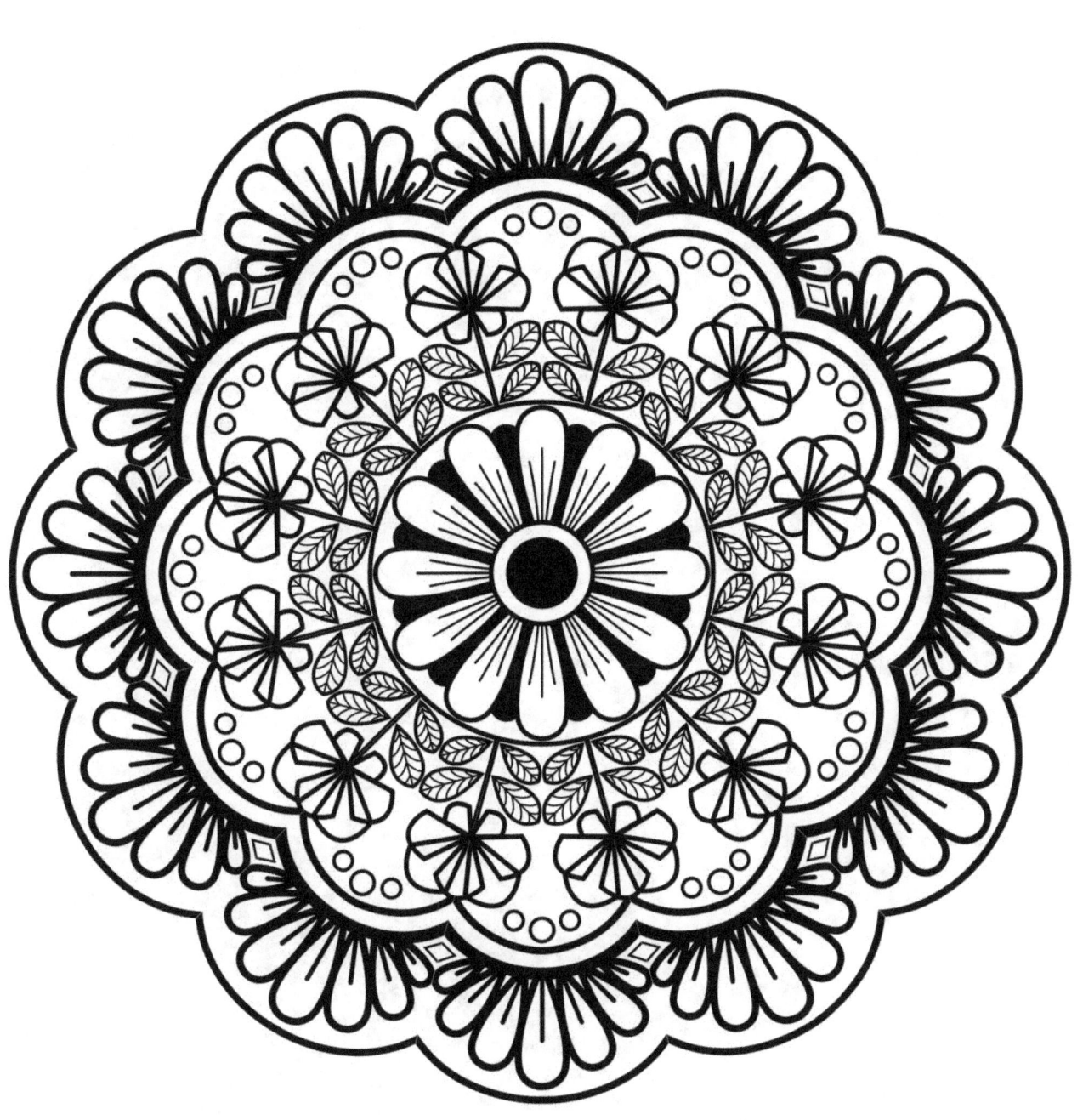

Thank you for purchasing our Coloring Book!
Please leave us a review on Amazon.

www.ingramcontent.com/pod-product-compliance
Lightning Source LLC
Chambersburg PA
CBHW081736220526

45468CB00008B/2122